NUMEROLOGY

Mastering The Secret Meanings Of Numbers In Your Life

By
Michelle Northrup

© Copyright 2019 by Michelle Northrup - All rights reserved.

This book is provided with the sole purpose of providing relevant information on a specific topic for which every reasonable effort has been made to ensure that it is both accurate and reasonable. Nevertheless, by purchasing this book you consent to the fact that the author, as well as the publisher, are in no way experts on the topics contained herein, regardless of any claims as such that may be made within. As such, any suggestions or recommendations that are made within are done so purely for entertainment value. It is recommended that you always consult a professional prior to undertaking any of the advice or techniques discussed within.

This is a legally binding declaration that is considered both valid and fair by both the Committee of Publishers Association and the American Bar Association and should be considered as legally binding within the United States.

The reproduction, transmission, and duplication of any of the content found herein, including any specific or extended information will be done as an illegal act regardless of the end form the information ultimately takes. This includes copied versions of the work both physical, digital and audio unless express consent of the Publisher is provided beforehand. Any additional rights reserved.

Furthermore, the information that can be found within the pages described forthwith shall be considered both accurate and truthful when it comes to freely available information and general consent. As such, any use, correct or incorrect, of the provided information will render the Publisher free of responsibility as to the actions taken outside of their direct purview. Regardless, there are zero scenarios where the original author or the Publisher can be deemed liable in any fashion for any damages or hardships that may result from any of the information discussed within.

Finally, any of the content found within is ultimately intended for entertainment purposes and should be thought of and acted on as such. Due to its inherently ephemeral nature nothing discussed within should be taken as an assurance of quality, even when the words and deeds described herein indicated otherwise. Trademarks and copyrights mentioned within are done for informational purposes in line with fair use and should not be seen as an endorsement from the copyright or trademark holder.

TABLE OF CONTENTS

INTRODUCTION 1
Chapter 1 *Numerology* 4
Chapter 2 *Calculating Your Personal Numerology* 9
Chapter 3 *Calculating Other Powerful Numbers* 23
Chapter 4 *Astrology* 31
Chapter 5 *The Zodiac* 54
Chapter 6 *Personal Astrology* 62
Chapter 7 *Tarot* 75
Chapter 8 *Forecasting And Divination* 95
Chapter 9 *How Numerology, Astrology And Tarot Are Connected* ... 102
Conclusion 107
Description 108

INTRODUCTION

Congratulations on purchasing *Numerology* and thank you for doing so.

The following chapters will discuss the way that numbers play an integral role in our lives as subtle influences and energies. Whether you acknowledge these energies or not they affect you in your day to day life. By working with these energies rather than ignore them, we can better understand our world and how to navigate it successfully.

Numbers are not only used to measure or keep track of the quantity of something, they also influence our lives through distinct patterns and meanings. In our modern, technologically advanced world many people believe or understand the relevance that numbers have in synchronistic events and 'coincidence'. Without acknowledging the power of numbers we cannot take advantage of their power to the fullest extent. Spiritual qualities of our existence are very mysterious, these subtle energies are not just out in the open for all to see. Many people spend their entire lifetimes seeking these influences, in hopes of discovering secrets about life that science cannot reveal alone. If you are reading this book then you may already have contemplated similar ideas and conceptions.

Many old cultures from around the world hold numbers in high spiritual regard, seeing them not only as symbols but as powerful influences with their own minds. It may seem far fetched to consider a number having intelligence, let alone power over aspects of our lives, but with some attention to detail and research we see that these ideas are common in all cultures up to just a couple hundred years ago. Consider the tangible power that numbers have, they are the basis of all science and technological growth, so why wouldn't they have some spiritual prowess?

In many cultures we see numbers that are considered unlucky, having the ability to frighten humans. We see numbers being used to measure the value of essentially everything, this must have some spiritual reaction, if even a subtle one. So where does one begin with working with numbers rather than against them?

Each number from 1 through 9 is thought to have a distinct personality, a certain way it behaves in our world. The subtle influence of these personalities is not something science seems to be concerned with and is often passed off as superstition with no place in our materialistic world. These behaviors take root in our tangible dimension through what many to be called 'luck', these instances of seemingly coincidental or impossible occurrences are the numbers syncing up into our lives in some of the more obvious ways. For the practitioner of numerology there are no coincidences.

With this ancient practice of numerology we see it inherent in more popular spiritual practices as well, namely astrology and tarot. These two crafts rely heavily on numbers to be useful for the student of occult practices. We see that the numbers and their personalities are used hand in hand with planets and the images of the tarot, this fact cannot be ignored. This brings up the idea that numerology is incomplete without a context to apply it to, but when there is a context the number's influence is usually extensive, if not the basis for many practices, spiritual or not. So how can we start to use numbers to our advantage?

This book aims to explore the power of numbers for beginners, covering numerology itself, as well as how it plays an integral role in astrology and tarot as well. In the subsequent chapters we will reveal the secrets of numbers and learn to apply them to our daily lives. These practices are some of the oldest occult sciences that are popular today. For beginners or intermediate practitioners alike, this book will fill in the gaps between numbers, astrology and the tarot. Read on to reintroduce the ancient skills our ancestors used to commune with the mysterious forces all around us.

While these practices have been widely lost in our modern world, there are many people who seek these mysteries. These ancient arts remain dormant in the popular culture's mind, waiting for individuals like yourself to peak beyond the veil of reality and harness the powers that belong to you. Even as you read right now you have begun your journey down a spiritual path, one that is transformative in nature and offers many treasures of human existence in its wake. Read thoroughly and always remember there is no one way that works for everyone, walk your own path.

There are plenty of books on this subject on the market, thanks again for choosing this one! Every effort was made to ensure it is full of as much useful information as possible, please enjoy!

CHAPTER 1
Numerology

The practice of numerology has been used since before written history. The mystics and wise men of this time were very familiar with the power held within numbers. They saw the patterns that were everywhere, from plants to stones to their own bodies. As you read on be aware of the patterns in your life, and the numbers that create them.

Defining Numerology

Using numbers to better navigate your human experience can come in many forms and practices. Many people use the patterns to make major decisions, whether it's investing or proposing to a significant other. For this book we will be looking at how to apply numerology to our personal lives and how it can strengthen our spiritual bonds with the world around us, thus communing with the mysterious divine. This idea presents the notion that numbers are imbedded with ties to events that take place in our lives. In the traditional models ancient students of this practice game numerical value to almost every aspect of life even names, words, animals and humans themselves.

These ancient students came to the conclusion that there truly are only nine numbers. These numbers are 1, 2,3,4,5,6,7,8 and 9, respectively. Any other number is just a repeat of the original nine numbers, thus 10 is 1+0 which equals 1. This simple math is the basis of numerology, simply adding the digits of any number together will eventually lead to a single digit which is the true nature of that number, hence 10 is a 1. By adding up any given sequence of numbers you will see a pattern of single digits. This pattern is simply the single digits repeating themselves; 10=1, 11=2, 12=3 and so on.

Example of calculation: the number 239; 2+3+9=14, 1+4=5, therefore 239 is a 5.

This calculation is quite simple but at the same time yields patterns that are mind blowing. Numbers with more than one digit are under the influence of these digits, but overall the sum of the digits gives you the main influential number, the essence of the larger number.

Many beginners have questions about the number zero. In numerology zero has no value, its zero. Zero is a concept that many ancient cultures did not use, zero has no beginning or end, it is nothing. Zero is not considered a number for intents and purposes here. When calculating numerological values zero still equals zero.

The simple calculations above are the main way to find out the numerology of someone or something, learn it by heart and expect to use it later.

History of Numerology

Numerology as an actual word has only been in use since 1907 in English. The Victorian era saw a huge surge in popularity for numerology, although it was not always used to commune with the divine. Many people of that era simply found it fun and intriguing to know so much about a person's personality with a single digit. Aside from somewhat recent English history, numerology was practiced centuries before Victoria.

There's no question that numerology or similar practices were used by our ancestors for centuries before contemporary times, but trying to find its exact beginnings is a lost cause. It is safe to say that numerology was practiced centuries before written word or our oldest discovered relics of lost cultures. In the very least numerology was used for spiritual practice within the scope of astrology. Our earliest records of the practice can be found in ancient Babylon known as the Chaldean system. Other ancient civilizations such as Egypt and Eastern Asia cultures have documented proof of numerology used for spiritual purposes.

It is hard to say how much these civilizations relied on numerology in their daily spiritual practice, perhaps they saw no difference between numbers in the tangible world and the numbers of spiritual realms. However prominent the practice was they most certainly used numbers to find ways to commune with the divine.

Numerological practices today are considered to be based wholly on the works of Pythagoras. The Greek philosopher's outstanding work with mathematics and numbers hold influence over math standards even in today's age. Pythagoras believed that numbers played a role in every aspect of our lives, every relationship and every encounter. He felt that contemplation of numbers and mathematics was crucial in developing a strong mind, and seeing subtle relationships between everything in the universe.

As the timeline continues we see numerology condemned by the Christian church, along with other spiritual practices including tarot and astrology. These powerful arts were technically thought of as 'magic' and thus dubbed evil deeds. With the suppression of magical arts, many seekers were forced to practice privately and the popularity of numerology slowly disappeared.

As the Victorian era approached numerology had its fifteen minutes of fad fame as Victorians calculated each other's numerological value like a parlor game. Soon other spiritual models came along with this revival, Theosophy and ceremonial magic groups like the Golden Dawn began thriving, and numerology along with them. This magical revival ushered in the 20th century with Aleister Crowley's teachings breaking through into public attention, and magic itself became something widely accepted across the western world.

As the 1960s and 1970s counterculture grew, alternative beliefs and lifestyles were being practiced all across Europe and America. Astrology, tarot and numerology became popular practices to explore, but inevitably saw their popularity fall and be left to small groups of dedicated practitioners and niche crowds for a few decades.

Today we see modern occult practices making yet another resurgence. The advent of the internet has made it easier than ever to explore many methods of communion with the divine. People share techniques and experiences that are building magical connections faster than ever before. The abundance of occult related religions and world views make it easy to find a fitting group for almost anyone. New Age, Neo Pagan, Wiccan and atheists alike have found places numerological practices within their belief systems and improve their understanding of the world.

Science may not be able to test numerological practices in the lab to see how it really works, but no spiritual practice can. Science is very valuable but cannot explain everything, although it tries to. Keep in mind that if you find a practice that works for you, then it works. Does it really matter how or why? The fact that it works is reason enough to accept it regardless of why. Be open minded as you form your new perspectives on the true nature of reality. Numbers hold power and these forces influence our lives every single day. If we can learn to notice them or even use them to our advantage, we can discover one of the many secrets of the universe. Improving our lives is the ultimate goal of using these practices. Many may just tap into a spiritual current for an instance to attain something they desire, this is not recommended. Once you start down this path there is no turning back, you have presented yourself to these forces and ignoring them from this point often brings negative consequences.

It's popular in modern culture to calculate your numerology online and have a look at what it says about your personality, this harmless enough. This is not a practice of the art and not privy to negative blowback if the practice is abandoned. This vague venture into the occult art is akin to how many treat astrology, only learning their sun sign and that's it. These practices are much more complex and if you intend to take the craft seriously, then it is suggested that you avoid umbrella terms and lazy approaches to these powerful forces.

CHAPTER 2
Calculating Your Personal Numerology

Let's move on to calculating your personal numbers. Using the techniques above to reduce the numbers to a single digit you can quickly learn your important numbers and build a better relationship with them. While these numbers aren't going to define who you are as a person today, they offer some insight into you natural behavioral makeup. Numbers do have influence but there are many other forces at work as well. Once you learn your numbers you can learn about their behaviors and see how they directly influence you and your life.

You will learn that your numerology is closely linked to your personal astrology, we will explore this in greater detail in later chapters. As you explore your own personal numbers you will see how they relate to each other, and eventually see how they relate to the other numbers. With time and dedication you will then know each number quite well, anticipating their influence and working with them to improve your life.

Calculating your numerology

As we mentioned above, calculating these numbers is quite easy. Sure, obtaining the number is simple but don't get too comfortable, the behaviors of the number is the complex part. Just like any relationship, there will be trial and error, mistakes and learning experiences. But through this treacherous experience we gain wisdom and find ways to navigate the relation with ease.

There are infinite different calculations you can do that pertain to the many aspects of life, but there are typically three main calculations that hold the most influence over our lives; Destiny number, the psychic number and the name number. Most any tradition of numerological teachings adhere to these main three numbers. Let's explore each number in detail.

Destiny Number

This number represents how you are seen by the world. This outsider's perspective sees how you carry yourself, how you look and overall just the way people see you. As you grow and gain life experience this number becomes more influential.

While the destiny number is prominent throughout your life, it really takes hold during the middle of your life, ages 40 to 45 and onward. Midlife crisis is often attributed to these dramatic changes. The destiny number is considered the most important number to build a relationship with since it's the 'matured' influence.

The destiny number is calculated by adding together the numbers of your birthday, birth year and birth month. For example if you are born August 19, 1979 you would add August's number, 8 plus the day 19, and the year 1979.

Example: $8+1+9+1+9+7+9=44$

The sum is 44. Now add together these digits.

$4+4=8$

For this example the birth date in question equals to a destiny number of 8. At this point we could explore the personality of 8 and research the aspects of life that number 8 influences. Think about your life and how 8 has come into play, certain years that add up eight like 2006 or days such as the 8th or 17th may be significant days for the qualities of 8 to be intensified.

Psychic Number

The calculation of the psychic number is another popular technique to practice numerology. This number is indicative of how you may look at yourself. This proverbial mirror influences how you judge your accomplishments and how you think you are.

This may or may not be how others see you. Your natural abilities like talents and interests are symbolic of the psychic number. This number is very influential during younger years, puberty to middle age.

Psychic numbers are calculated by adding the digits of your birth day together. So keeping with the above example, if you were born August 19 you would add the digits 1 and 9.

$$\text{Example: } 1+9=10, 1+0=1$$

For this example your psychic number would be 1. Consider your youth and any '1' influences. Major events at age 10 or days that are 'ones' like the 1st, 10th or 28th. This number will reveal any dormant special talents you may not be aware, or even give insight into your youthful past.

Name Number

When calculating the name number it gets to be slightly more complicated. This number is the essence of the vibration of your name. Consider the fact that you hear your name all through your life, this sound surely has an effect on you in some way. This number is often represented by your relationships with people. Not only romantic relationships but any encounter with other people, so fellow employees, people you see on occasion and people that you see often.

This number is quite different than the other two main numerical values we are working with. Many people change their name or are given nicknames, this will alter your name number, and in turn change which number is influencing your relationships with others. Even changing a last name during marriage can have dramatic effects on this influence, for better or worse. If you do not have a favorable name number it's easily changed to a more beneficial one. Many people change their names or are assigned new names when they have a spiritual awakening or are initiated into a spiritual or religious group. Some people change their name to detach from a religious affiliation. When changing your name choose wisely and calculate the number that will work well with your other numerology,

Calculating the name number requires a set alphabetical system that has assigned values to each letter, then you add the values of the letters in your name. There are many different alphabetical systems. Below are the three main alphabetical systems translated into English.

Latin Alphabetical System

1 – a, j, s   2 – b, k, t   3 – c, l, u

4 – d, m, v   5 – e, n, w   6 – f, o, x

7 – g, p, y   8 – h, q, z   9 – i, r

Vedic Alphabetical System

1 – a, I, j, q, y   2 – b, k, r   3 – c, g, l, s

4 – d, m, t   5 – e, h, n, x   6 – u, v, w

7 – o, z   8 – f, p   9 – i, r

Pythagorean Alphabetical System

1 – a, j, s   2 – b, k, t   3 – c, l, u

4 – d, m, v   5 – e, n, w   6 – f, o, x

7 – g, p, y   8 – h, q, z   9 – i, r, x

To calculate your name number just choose a fitting system above and use the values presented to calculate the letters of your name. We will use the Vedic system in the following example. Choose the name you hear most often or choose a nickname that is prominent in your life.

For this example we will calculate the value of the name Jonathan.

$$J=1, O=7, N=5, A=1, T=4, H=5, A=1, N=5$$

$$1+7+5+1+4+5+1+5=29$$

$$2+9=11$$

$$1+1=2$$

$$2$$

In this example Jonathan equal the numerological value of 2. With this number you could then go find out what the behaviors and attitudes of 2 are and apply them to your life. Does 2 work well with your other numerology? Would it be more beneficial to change your name? Think deeply about this before drastically altering your numerological makeup.

Now that we have learned to calculate our numerology we can explore the numbers as individuals. For each number there is a set of behaviors and certain aspects of life that they influence. There is also a color, planet, day, stones and many other characteristics that are ascribed to any given number. By learning the attributes of each number you can better navigate your life with ease.

Numbers 1 through 9

Familiarizing ourselves with the behavior of the numbers will take some time. You are not expected to memorize all the numbers immediately, a good place to start is to learn the three numbers that influence you the most. These numbers are not only influencing you individually but work together to form relationships and further complicated influences that are more subtle. Take your destiny, psychic and name number and check the chart below to learn their qualities and behaviors. Learn these numbers by heart and keep a close eye out for synchronicities as these numbers influence your life from here on out.

One

Color: Gold, Yellow / Planet: Sun / Day: Sunday

Destiny: For a destiny number 1 represents leadership roles, this number's influence is motivated and self-sustaining. Having success in the material world is a huge motivator for this number. Personal goals are very important and self-worth is measured by material success. Number 1 is energetic and creative, being able to solve problems easily and bravely face challenges. This intense leadership can have negative effects that manifest as controlling attitudes or narcissism.

Psychic: For a psychic number, 1 is confident and joyous, seemingly never running out of energy at times. This number is often considered a lucky number for psychic influence. Although if unbalanced this influence can lead to distracted mindsets or over ambitious attitudes.

Name: For a name number, 1 aims to be self-reliant and self-sustainable. Typically seeking a leadership role, this influence boasts creativity and problem solving skills. Running a small business or working in the arts are often fitting careers for name number 1.

Two

Color: White, Silver / Planet: Moon / Day: Monday

Destiny: For a destiny number, 2 offers diplomatic skills and a need to achieve something that impacts the world in a positive way.

Compassion and understanding are key with this destiny number. The ability to negotiate and keep the peace are favorable skills, but can also be used for negative reasons such as selfish gain. Many destiny number 2 people have a greater sense of spiritual insight and understanding.

Psychic: For a psychic number, 2 offers sensitivity and empathy towards others. This makes for selfless socializing and meaningful friendships. Destiny number 2 often have to do things twice to get the job done.

Name: For a name number, 2 offers a sense of needed action to change the world. Striving to find spiritual understanding and promote humanitarian causes makes name number 2 people excellent for charitable work and ministry activities. Philosophy and teaching are common careers for name number 2 influences. If unbalanced anxiety and lack of self-worth can be prominent, especially if these influences don't have a meaningful outlet.

Three
Color: Yellow / Planet: Jupiter / Day: Thursday

Destiny: For a destiny number, 3 influences the creative faculties in a great way, offering artistic ideas and ease of expression whether it's through art, speaking or other means. This number's influence is optimistic and often looks at the brighter side of life. This can potentially be a negative thing if one cannot recognize negativity and learn from it. Destiny 3 people love to entertain and always makes sure their guests or friends are having a good time.

Psychic: For a psychic number, 3 offers resilience and stamina. Mental readiness and physical quickness are greatly influenced by this number. Psychic 3 people are often restless and need an outlet to release this energy. If not effective vented this energy can lead to exhaustion and disorganization.

Name: For a name number, 3 needs artistic outlets or other means to vent the abundant optimistic energies. These people tend to live in the moment often going from place to place or job to job. Many 3 name number people enter into the entertainment business or creative consulting. These people also tend to maintain long friendships and hold on to companions for life.

Four

Color: Gold / Planet: Uranus/Rahu Day: Sunday

Destiny: For a life path number, 4 tends to have a skillful ability to construct. Whether literally constructing a structure or constructing a plan, destiny four people have a natural knack to build. This number also offers much in the way of calmness and balanced perspectives. These people are grounded and ready at a moment's notice to act on their plans.

Psychic: For a psychic number, 4 has an organizing quality, making responsibilities and dedication a driving factor. Destiny 4 people are practical and act rationally in the face of adversity. This may lead to hard headedness and the inability to work with others successfully

Name: For a name number, 4 aims to balance out and organize the chaos of the world. In a sense of servitude to their fellow man, name 4 people are determined to assist humanity progress to a more fair and balanced society. Many of these people find themselves in a career that is charitable or helps to build community, whether literally through construction of homes or figuratively by organizing potlucks or community events.

Five

Color: Green / Planet: Mercury / Day: Wednesday

Destiny: For a destiny number, 5 people are always thinking ahead. They tend to be progressive in their views and always one step ahead. This foresight is beneficial in many parts of life, but if left unbalanced can lead to lack of living in the moment. Deep and intricate thoughts prevail in the mind of the destiny 5 individual, which leads to the need to ask the big questions and seek their answers. Exploring the mysterious and unknown is common among destiny 5 influence.

Psychic: For a psychic number, 5 has an influence that gives someone a real sense of teamwork. Destiny number 5 people work very well with others and prefer to work in groups. This could potentially lead to lack of self-reliance if unbalanced. This number also adds skills in maintaining routines as well as a quick analytical mind especially while brainstorming with others.

Name: For a name number, 5 influences an individual to usher in big societal changes. They are frustrated as injustice and lack of freedom for underprivileged and minority groups. They often reach out to others in need and enter fields of work that influence the society they live in. Science, politics and environmentalism are careers that are suitable for this name number.

Six

Color: Blue, Indigo / Planet: Venus / Day: Friday

Destiny: For a destiny number, 6 is very influential on the aspect of parenting. Many destiny 6 people start large families or volunteer helping the underprivileged. These people are great at teaching young children and offering a fair perspective on the world, not sugar coating it. Kindness and abundant love are held in high regard. These people tend to see the beauty in everything and love sensual pleasures.

Psychic: For a psychic number, 6 influences an individual to have great domestic skills, often being very caring for their loved ones and the world around them. Fairness and justice are key aspects of this person's mindset. They tend to go out of their way to make sure others are doing well and have all that they need to survive.

Name: For a name number, 6 offers much in the way of love and affection. Often going out of their way to please others, these people love committed romantic relationships. Many name number 6 people work as counselors or chefs. This selflessness can potentially lead these people to be taken advantage of or relying on others to find value in their own lives.

Seven

Color: Blue / Planet: Neptune, Ketu / Day: Monday

Destiny: For a destiny number, 7 people are reserved and quiet until they can trust someone, then they become quite sociable. These people are great at getting to the heart of someone's true motives, using their excellent judge of character to size up any other people in the vicinity. Destiny 7 people have high expectations of their peers and expect logic and reason in their conversations.

Psychic: For a psychic number, 7 influences the capacity to observe in an unbiased way. These perceptive skills offer mindfulness and a sense of foresight. This number also has a lonely quality as it is not very trusting unless proven otherwise. If unbalanced this number is stubborn and disregards authority

Name: For a name number, 7 hunts relentless for truth within the world. Whether it's truth within themselves or truths that are held secret within the mysteries of our universe, they seek them. Introspective and observant, these people often work as teachers or study occult arts. The introspection that comes with name number 7 can sometimes lead one to be alone for long periods of time, this can be detrimental if left unbalanced.

Eight

Color: Black, Purple / Planet: Saturn / Day: Saturday

Destiny: For a destiny number, 8 is organized and great at governing situations with an unbiased perspective. They are ambitious and motivated mainly by material possessions and success. Challenges and tough goals are gladly accepted by these people, their hard working attitude can handle any major task in a timely manner.

Psychic: For a psychic number, 8 is logical and skillful in fair judgement. Material affairs are easily navigated since these people recognize the limitations of the material world and also know their own boundaries well. This materialist mindset could lead to greed or lack of spiritual awareness.

Name: For a name number, 8 needs to obtain material success or they feel worthless. Steady work and income are a necessity or the individual will be stressed and restless. Many name number 8 people find themselves owning a business or working their way up the corporate ladder working years for a big company. If unbalanced this number's influence can overexert its need for material success, leaving the individual unaware of spiritual realms and unable to see the value of love and other intangible things.

Nine

Color: Red / Planet: Mars / Day: Tuesday

Destiny: For a destiny number, 9 is generous offering their services to those in need. They are reliable and aim to change the world through their actions and attitude. Prideful and confident, destiny number 9 people despise hate and injustice, seeking to heal the world of these travesties. These people see themselves as having a duty to their fellow man to change the world for the better. These high standards inspire destiny number 9 people to work smarter and achieve their important goals.

Psychic: For a psychic number, 9 offers a natural drive that motivates and inspires. Humanitarian issues are very important and often is a driving force behind these people's actions. Psychic

9 people are open minded but not afraid to debate and try to convince others to agree with them.

Name: For a name number, 9 seeks to understand humanity to the fullest extent. They wish to know the hows and whys of human existence, aiming to take this knowledge and inspire the world around them. Many name number 9s find themselves having careers in the medical field, law and humanitarian fields. This sense of dedication to the world makes them good workers for any career that is honest and just.

More on the number nine:
9 is an unusual number when compared to the other numbers. Number 9 is the final number before the numbers begin repeating themselves, this makes the number a sort of gatekeeper to the next pattern. 9 is often seen as a number that is so influential that as a destiny number many traditions feel that the individual will evolve spiritually in a next life.

In numerology each number has an 'opposite number'. If two numbers add up to nine then they are opposites. For example: 2+7=9 therefore 2 and 7 are opposites. We notice here that the number 9 does not have an opposite, it stands alone as the final number in the repetitive patterns.

Another key point about 9 is that it cancels itself out when we are calculating our numerology. This is because any number added to 9 just reduces to itself. For example 2+9=11, 1+1=2. This makes the calculations easier, you can simply eliminate any 9 in your numerology and add the remaining numbers and get the correct number. For example:

$$\text{Birth date: } 10/19/1989$$

$$1+0+1+9+1+9+8+9=38$$

$$3+8=11$$

$$1+1=2$$

2 is the life path number.

Now let's eliminate the 9s

$$1+0+1+1+8=11$$

$$1+1=2$$

We see that 2 is our answer once again.

This easy shortcut can make calculating numerology just a bit easier, but also shows that 9 is a special number that doesn't work the same as the other numbers. This is very curious to the student of numerology, and lifetime can be spent recognizing patterns of 9s. In Indian numerology a 9x9 chart is drawn up and the numbers are reduced to single digits after being multiplied. If you were to connect all of any number distinct patterns are formed, it is thought that this is how intricate Indian textile patterns are designed. Each number and its respected opposite form shapes that mirror each other, but of course 9 does not have an opposite, and indeed we see in these charts that 9's shape is not symmetrical either. Here we learn that 9 is very important as it relates to other numbers.

We have now explored each digit individually and familiarized ourselves with their attributes and behaviors. It is best to keep in mind that all the numbers work together as major influences in our lives, simply because we have a destiny number of 3 doesn't mean that 3 is the only influence. It is recommended that you look at all the numbers and get to know them. Learn how they are interrelated and how they act towards one another. This will help you see the patterns all around you as well as prepare you for any intensified influence these numbers may present in the future, whether beneficial or detrimental.

With the basics of numerology in our mind, let's take a look at other popular numerological calculations and use of numbers in our day to day lives. While the three calculations listed above are the most influential, other numbers and calculations affect the more subtle aspects of our lives.

CHAPTER 3
Calculating Other Powerful Numbers

Numbers go on infinitely, you can literally count for an entire lifetime and not run out of numbers to calculate. We have seen the influence each number has, and how they behave within certain aspects of our lives. The techniques you learned in the previous chapter go a long way in exploring the world of numerology, but there are other uses for these numbers as well.

Depending on the culture there are many numbers that hold various prowess, whether they are lucky or unlucky, are signs of coming tragedy or even signs of worldly events like dangerous whether or wars. There are many ways to use these numbers. If you have an unbalanced numerology, find the numbers that are opposites of your numbers and work with them by choosing favorable days to plan big events, or wearing the suitable color of the number. The possibilities are endless in the ways you can work with these numbers. Many skilled practitioners of numerology use numbers to forecast the future, even being able to affect the future if they are skilled enough. This divination is not unlike astrology and tarot, more details on these arts in later chapters.

Let's take a look at techniques and powerful numbers and how we can use them to improve our lives.

Inspirational Numbers

Inspirational and motivational numbers are somewhat new practices in numerology, they can be calculated by adding up the value of only the vowels in your name. This number typically influences your hidden desires that you yourself may not even be aware of. Often when exploring this number fears arise and can be faced in a healthy way. These numbers can be very helpful to explore if you have emotional blockages or other obstacles.

Below are the numbers 1-9 listed and their correspondences to inspirational and motivational numbers.

1

This number influences your desire to be selfish and uppity. You may have feelings of superiority towards others, and want to have it your way most of the time. You have the answers and they are not up for discussion. Examining this number in you numerology can help you better understand and combat these negative habits.

2

This number influences the need for rest and relaxation. Keeping a peaceful social life and drama-free workplace are crucial to you. Routines and close knit friends or family are ideal. Working with this number can help balance this out, whether you need more chaos in your life or more peace.

3

This number influences desires to be in the public eye. Whether it's celebrity or just a few minutes in the spotlight you may have an unhealthy infatuation with this perspective. Your popularity is important to you, and you Gauge your self-worth on your popularity. Working with numbers can help you combat these negative habits.

4

This number influences your need to have everything structured and planned out. There is no sense of spontaneity or adventure, everything has to be put into certain arrangements and you cannot stand a surprise. You believe it is your duty to arrange and structure everything around you. Analyzing number 4 can help you loosen this grip, and combat these negative habits.

5

This number influences your desire to constantly be moving and changing. This behavior gives you a sense of freedom as you are able to move at your own pace and without regard to responsibilities or other people's needs. Constant adventure and fun, stimulation and excess all come with this territory. Work with number 5 to help balance these negative patterns.

6

This number influences your need to live a perfectly balanced life, free of challenges or confrontation. Avoiding arguments and never pushing yourself to new heights is preferred. You tend to give into others and be taken advantage of to avoid sticking up for yourself. Work with number 6 to help combat this negative habit, and find the value of asserting yourself.

7

This number influences your desire to be alone and accomplish things on your own. You wish to be alone and take credit for all your accomplishments as if you had no assistance or teaching. You push away your loved ones to focus on your personal endeavors. Use number 7 to help combat these detrimental habits and open up to teamwork or help in general.

8

This number influences your desire for wealth in the material world. You are only motivated by material gains and gauge your success by how much you accumulate. You must have the newest technologically advanced devices and cars, and boast about your gains. Combat this unhealthy habit by balancing out your relationship with number 8.

9

This number influences your desire to achieve spiritual or religious success. You desperately search for truth in spiritual teachings and books to the point of obsession, often missing the point of the studies in general. You feel so strongly that you go out of your way to focus in on the spiritual side of life, ignoring earthly affairs. Combat this negative habit by working with number 9.

Love Numbers

Relationship numerology is practiced mainly using destiny numbers, when two people have favorable life path numbers then they may have a long and healthy relationship, platonic or romantic. For a general rule life path numbers that are opposites have different viewpoints but this allows room to change and grow within a relationship, this is generally quite challenging but rewarding. Life path numbers that the same generally have similar interests and desires, but can become stagnant with little change or growth. We see a distinct balance between these two concepts, neither are good or bad.

You can generally look at any two number's attributes and think about what kind of combination they may create, below we will discuss each number as it pertains to relationships and compatibility.

1

This number enjoys being the leader in a relationship, they feel that they can control the relationship and steer it into a successful direction. This can be troublesome if someone is overly controlling or too strict. Generally love number 1 people need a physical outlet and some sense of growth in a relationship.

2

This number loves sharing their relationship duties 50/50. They see a partnership as being a two way street and each person within it needs to contribute their fair share. This can be troublesome if someone becomes too clingy or needy. Generally love number 2 people are empathetic and affectionate.

3

This number creates a shell around people that makes them appear not interested in relationships, although under the shell the individual actually desires commitment. Compatibility is important to this number since they need someone who can crack their shell and get to their heart. Generally love number 3 people need assurance and foundation in a relationship.

4

This number is dedicated in relationships, with a high tolerance for drama or adversity. They need structure and consistency in a relationship and at times can be too passive. Generally love number 4 people are adventurous and reliable.

5

This number requires transparency and open communication in their partnerships. They tend to not hold anything back during fights and are truthful. This honesty can be offensive at times but love number 5 people will always be committed and keep their word.

6

This number is well known for its relationship to sex and beauty. People with this love number love sensual pleasures and romanticism. They love cooking and catering to their lover and like that behavior to be reciprocated. These high standards are tough to meet, but generally love number 6 people are open and caring.

7

This number is associated with the mystery side of love. Spiritual companionship is desired and shared goals of spiritual growth are ideal for these people. Generally love number 7 people are intense and thoughtful.

8

This number is logical and structured in relationships. They seek stability and a firm foundation to build upon. Financial security is a must and sometimes can get in the way of the relationship. Generally love number 8 people are reliable and responsible.

9

This number is very mature within relationships, they are insightful and have lots of experience. They desire mental clarity and intelligence in a lover and must be working to great goals of environmentalism or humanitarian ideas. Generally this love number is eccentric and knowledgeable.

Prosperous Numbers

It's quite common for people to find their way into a numerology practice when they are in need of money. As with trying so many other 'get rich quick' schemes hasn't worked, numerology isn't going to make you rich overnight. But it can help you find paths that will lead to more money if used correctly. Consider choosing lines of work that are in line with your numerological makeup. Planning certain job interviews on favorable days may help you get the job. There are many ways of applying numerology to these important financial choices. View it as not guaranteeing your success but increasing the odds of your success, if even a little bit.

1

This number is great for financial gain, many people who have a destiny number 1 have success in their careers. Working with the number 1 can help immensely in your pursuit of success. Choose days that are '1s' to plan job hunting or to start a new business, days that add to 1 would be 1, 10, 19, or 28.

2

This number is considered detrimental to financial success in many traditions. The number 2 often causes tasks to have to be done twice, therefore delaying your success or advancement. Numbers like 11 and 22 are influenced greatly by 2 and are recognized as wealthy numbers, but not necessarily for money. With this in mind do not start or attempt to finish projects on days that are '2s'; 2, 11, 20, 29.

3

This number can be good for gaining monetary wealth, but only through dedication and hard work. If this number is heavy in you numerological makeup than you may have to work hard and long at something to see profits. Shopping sprees should be avoided and investing is recommended to get the most out of 3 for financial reasons.

4

This number is great for ensuring employment for long periods of time. People who cannot keep jobs for long will benefit greatly from working with 4. Days that are '4s' are great for asking for raises or promotions; 4, 8, 13, 22, 31

5

This number is relatively neutral when dealing with finances. Although if someone has heavy 5 influence in their numerological makeup they may be partial to travel, so it is recommended to spend wisely and plan trips meticulously.

6

This number is helpful when you are seeking to invest or save for the future. Any financial dealings for mid to late life can be assisted by 6. Opening bank accounts and savings accounts in the days that are '6s' is recommended; 6, 15, 24.

7

This number can influence in a positive or negative way with finances. It is not recommended that this influence be called upon for monetary gain since it is risky. Although the rare times that 7 is helpful it is helpful in very profitable ways. Consider 7's role in gambling, it can give instant riches or take them away.

8

This number is helpful for prosperity in many ways. Its influence helps to organize spending and savings, as well as offering logical decision making when it comes to careers. Deadlines will be met, hard work will pay off and monetary gains will come. This is a pretty straight forward number to work with, you do the work and you will receive benefits. Number 8 also pairs well with number 2 to balance time management.

Keep in mind that 8 does not like it when you agree to something and don't fulfill your end of the deal, so be careful not to slack off or be unfair in business adventures when working with 8.

9

This number can be confusing when it comes to finances. The 9 energy is constantly attracting wealth of all kinds, while also disregarding material desire at the same time. This may result in quick, moderate sums of money, but will typically be answered with surprise bills or spending.

11 and 22

The numbers 11 and 22 get their own special recognition since many traditions of numerology hold these numbers in high regard as special. These master numbers are thought to offer spiritual insight and awareness if they are heavy in your numerology. Some people even feel that these people are destined to be of service to humanity, and assist with the spiritual progress of humanity. This leads these people to have paranormal experiences and strange occurrences that result in spontaneous adventure. This can be troublesome if someone is unaware of these forces.

While this seems like a lot of pressure to be put onto someone we need to keep in mind that their contribution to the spiritual progress of humanity can be in many different forms. Whether big or small these influences are to be taken seriously. Consult with experts or knowledgeable teachers about these numerological combinations if you have had any intense experiences regarding spiritual realms and are heavily influenced by 11 or 22.

CHAPTER 4
Astrology

For millennia humans have looked to the stars to better understand our world and find meaning in a chaotic universe. The art of astrology has been practiced by humans for all of written history and naturally even before our earliest written records. Ancient ruins and artifacts have proven that astrology has had a great influence on the evolution of humanity. Knowledge from the heavens have influenced our sense of time and calendars, our religious growth and some of the greatest mysteries of our lives.

Complicated astrological practices and techniques have been discovered in India, China, South America and many other ancient cultures. The stars were a crucial part of every human's life up until only a few hundred years ago. The advent of technological advancement and scientific thinking have weakened the emphasis on stars in exchange for more materialistic ideas. This essentially eliminates a fundamental reality about the progression of humanity on earth, we had a relationship with the heavens that have recently been abandoned.

Defining Astrology
The relationship we have with the stars and planets holds many secrets concerning our existence, spirituality and the universe as a whole. The Hermetic slogan of 'as above so below' is a foundational philosophy found in many religions around the world. This saying references the idea that activities in heaven are mirrors to activity on Earth, whether symbolically or literally. The attributions and behaviors of the planets are similar to the way numbers behave as well, but on a more observable scale. These planets influence events on earth and can be studied to harness their powers or predict future events. While science has no interest in astrology it has not been proven how these influences occur, perhaps it can't be

proven. All the while our ancient ancestors and astrologers today have spoken of their success with their astrology practices.

The major step for beginners in astrology is to learn their natal charts. These charts document the position of the planets at the exact moment you are born. The position of the planets and the constellations they are in give insight into one's life events and their personality. These charts are similar to numerological makeup in the sense that while natal charts show a lot about your natural makeup, other factors come into play as well.

This insight into personality traits and life events is useful, but one other major aspect of astrology is timing. You can effectively time events and plans to certain astrological events to ensure success. Consider societies before technology or even calendars, they used the stars to know when harvest season was coming, or when to have festivals that would be successful. This astrological timing was crucial to working with natural forces and ensure success for the societies. These practices still work today, and are some of the easiest and most practical applications of astrology for our day and age.

Before the invention of the telescope humans could only see as far as Saturn, ancient maps of the zodiac show this and contain glyphs and myths that are still valued today as powerful knowledge. These stories and glyphs have been used for thousands of years, right up to today. Potentially mapping the heavens can offer insight into all aspects of the human experience, even as it shifts and changes with the times.

As technology advances our universe grows as we can now perceive past Saturn and into the far reaches of space even outside our solar system. This complicates astrology and add further mystery, not unlike our world on earth as it gets more complicated the more science discovers.

Astrology may be complicated, but even beginners can feel its power with only a few first steps. Even the simplest practice yields grand results and opens your perspective to the heavens. It will do anyone good to look up from our screens and into the skies.

History of Astrology

Scientifically astrology can be proven to have been used since the 2nd millennium BCE. It can be safely assumed that the art was used before this time as well. Even as a general way to keep track of time the activity in the skies was crucial. The relationship humans have with the heavens was taken very seriously, if an out of the ordinary event occurred, such as an eclipse, it was seen as an ominous sign. This symbolically charged lifestyle was potent with spiritual power and potential, today we find the same mysteries and power, but many see it as superstition.

Our ancestors looked to the night sky for guidance, cave paintings even show celestial bodies, seeming to be a way to keep track of the events. Moon cycles and eclipses are some of the earliest recordings of astrology practices. Once humans settled and invented agriculture they used the stars to keep track of harvest times and planting times for their crops. The pyramids of Giza and other temples seem to align with certain constellations during auspicious times of the year for spiritual practice or ritual.

The earliest known recording of astrology was found in Mesopotamia and even seems to resemble Greek and Roman astrology which is widely used as the foundation of modern astrological practices. Although these systems are on two different continents they both utilize similar tools such as the zodiac, trine aspects and planetary rulers for certain zodiac signs. We see here that the heavens have a universal approach regardless of location on earth.

The rising power of the Christian church in the not so distant past saw astrology persecuted and outlawed, although the bible itself is filled with start mythology and astrological symbolism. The renaissance helped astrology became more widespread only to be counteracted by the Enlightenment period which viewed astrology as superstition. As the Victorian era came the magical revival supported the return of astrology into the popular sphere, especially horoscopes, which tend to be more for fun than actual practice.

In all centuries even leading up to our own we see astrological themes in art, literature and music. The stars were key in every aspect of life, astrology was even considered a science until astronomy took its place. With all the greatest minds of written history using astrology it surely has some validity with or without science. These inspiring minds quite literally would invoke the planets to imbue their work with power, allowing themselves to only be catalysts to the incredible power of the heavens.

This ancient history of astrology may be somewhat mysterious and complex, but it cannot simply be ignored. We base our modern day success on the great artists and thinkers of ancient Greece and Rome, why not also upkeep their practices within the sphere of astrology? If there is a powerful potential in our relationship with the heavens then we should maintain this relation and not ignore these forces.

Modern astrology is fraught with misconception and many contradictory ideas. Social media makes it tough to navigate the current astrological culture, but there are legitimate astrologers out there with all the information available, choose wisely who you listen to. And as always do what works for you, not what everyone else is doing.

The Planets

The planets within our solar system are the most influential bodies in our astrological makeup. When we refer to planets we also include the moon and sun, although they are not technically planets. These planets symbolize almost every aspect of human life, mirroring the behaviors of humans themselves. Personality traits found in humans can be attributed to a certain planetary influence. Consider when you are in a bad mood for no reason, just an uncomfortable feeling form out of nowhere. This could very well be attributed to unfavorable placement of planets at the moment or throughout that day. Perhaps it's Mars transiting your natal mars, which is placed in a detrimental position in the zodiac.

As planets dance throughout the zodiac they create combinations of influences and energies as complex as the human psyche, some are felt very intensely, others are more subtle. These influences can be navigated with some dedicated work, rather than just bombarding you with intense emotion and circumstances. By paying attention to the planets we can keep track of their influences, prepare ourselves for any intense changes and essentially move with the planets rather than against them. The closer a planet appears to earth the greater the influence. The moon and sun are obviously more influential since they literally sustain life on earth.

As we navigate the complex terrain of the heavens we can eventually learn to use their influence to our advantage. By building this relationship with the planets we gain insight not only into our personal lives but also the world around us. With a little dedication and work we can begin this journey to reacquaint ourselves with the heavens. Let's look at each major celestial body in detail.

Sun

Day: Sunday / Number: 1 / Exalted in Aries

The hub of our solar system, the sun is the closest star to earth and the energy source for life on earth. We know today that the sun is the middle of the solar system we live in, but from our perspective here on earth it appears to move across the sky, forming intricate patterns and dancing with the moon. Our calendar, the Gregorian calendar, is based on the sun's journey through the zodiac.

The sun represents the driving force that powers all nature, including human behavior. It represents the ego and our energetic essence, governing decision making, inspiration and motivation. The sun's placement in the zodiac is a general and vague overview of who you are as a whole. It is like a foundation that the other planet's influence can build upon. The sun sign is the central core of your astrological makeup.

Sun sign astrology is popular in the form of horoscopes. We find these in popular magazines and websites frequently. These are all based on general sun sign influence combined with the constellation's general influence. While we find great use in the sun sign's influence, it is important to know how it relates to other planets, rather than just the sun's vague influence.

Moon

Day: Monday / Number: 2 / Exalted in Taurus

The moon is the closest planet to the earth, in fact revolving around the earth. This makes its influence very important in earthly life. The moon is seen as a mirror, reflecting the sun's light and offering humanity a look into their own existence. Emotions, subconscious habits and self-image are governed by the moon's influence. The moon moves quickly across the sky, taking only 29 days to journey through the zodiac. This fluid motion is indicative of the moon's behavior. She controls the waters of the oceans, and generally influences constant change.

The slowly grows full and then recedes into darkness during her cycles, a symbolic life, death and rebirth. There are thirteen moon cycles in a solar year, each one having a different influence as it waxes and wanes across the night sky. She is mysterious and yet at the right moments offers insight into our lives and the universe.

The moon is typically representative of fertility and female energies, many believe the menstruation cycles to be governed by the moon, hormones themselves regulated by her influence. Many festivals are held on full moons, and other auspicious lunar nights. The moon cannot be ignored, nor is it wise to do so.

Mars

Day: Tuesday / Number: 9 / Exalted in Capricorn

This red planet is frequently compared to Venus since it has a fiery and masculine quality. Mars governs malefic and aggressive energies that are inherent in all living things. This energy at its worst is responsible for wars and violent acts all around the world. Sex drive, aggression and fiery passion are all aspects of Mars influence.

Taking action in general can also attributed to Mars, depending on its placement in your chart you may be assertive in social situations or the workplace. On the opposite end you Mars placement may give you a more reserved approach to taking action. It's recommended to keep an eye on Mars transits or when Mars is retrograde. These intense placements can conjure aggressive behavior and combative attitudes. During these times intensive exercise or other outlets can be a healthy way to channel Mars energy.

Mercury

Day: Wednesday / Number: 5 / Exalted in Virgo

Mercury governs travel and communication. Intelligent and rhythmic thinking are also signs of this quick moving planet's balanced influence. Mercury has a tendency to have a trickster nature, moving quickly through different signs and presenting spontaneous obstacles. Witty and influential, mercurial energies come across welcoming and yet can change dramatically quite quickly. Restlessness and overstimulation can be more likely if you have a heavy mercurial influence.

Mercury is quite popular for its retrograde activity. Mercury goes into retrograde frequently and tends to cause trouble for many people when doing so. These times are fraught with car troubles, communication issues and delays in everything. It's smart to have an outlet for these energies during these retrograde patterns, and is not recommended that any important business is started during mercury retrograde. Travel also may get hindered during these times, losing car keys and other items is also more likely.

Jupiter

Day: Thursday / Number: 3 / Exalted in Cancer

This benefic gaseous planet is widely attributed to prosperity and success. Optimistic and joyous, Jupiter was a favorite of old kings and other rulers seeking wealth and long life. As the largest planet in our solar system Jupiter has a commanding attitude toward other planets, often adding a positive ingredient to the mix. If placed favorably this planet can bring luck and material wealth that comes with ease.

Higher education, worldly truths and progressive concepts are attributed to Jupiter. Friend of this planet have an adept philosophical outlook that is very 'glass half full'. The ideals of this planet are set in stone so when approaching his energy be very humble and prove your selflessness to him. Hard work will be needed to work with this energy, expect to spend lots of time focused on his behavior.

Jupiter can travel the entire zodiac in twelve years, somewhat slow moving this is indicative of the time it takes to do the work to get the desired reward, optimism is needed during these trying times of long hours and commitment. It's easy to become self-involved and narcissistic when successfully working with Jupiter be sure to give credit where credit is due.

Venus

Day: Friday / Number: 6 / Exalted in Pisces

Venus is well known for its governance over beauty and love. This planet goes a long way in shaping our desires, offering affectionate attentiveness or even obsession. This is often taken as a sexual behavior but desires can be for almost anything. Chocolate, jewelry and clothing are popular indulgences that can become excessive, especially with a heavy Venus influence. What attracts you and what is attracted to you are governed by Venus as well, having an unfavorable placement of this planet can cause you to attract troubles like negative self-image and eating disorders. Many of your favorite things are influenced by Venus, music, foods, movies and other art are all influenced by Venus.

While Venus gets a lot of attention for sexual energy, other planets affect sex as well. Venus will more so affect what 'gets you in the mood' and your relationship with sex in a general sense. Your sex appeal and sexual preferences are influenced by Venus as well. Many people believe that if you are female then you will use the Venus energy to attract your significant others, and if you are male then you are using the Venus energy to discover what type of woman attracts you.

Venus has a very distinct relationship with the sun. Wherever the sun is placed in your natal chart Venus will be close by, either in the same sign or to a connecting sign. Venus is often the first celestial body that is seen in the morning and is also one of the first planets you see in the evening sky. For this reason we give Venus the titles of morning start or evening star respectively.

Saturn
Day: Saturday / Number: 8 / Exalted in Libra

Saturn is the most distant planet that the human eye can see without help from a telescope. This malefic planet is often seen as a negative influence as it governs death, time and limitations. This negative label is unjustified since Saturn teaches us many lessons that are crucial for growth and understanding of the human experience. Saturn also has an important influence over the other planets, imposing limitation and boundaries over their influences.

Because of this Saturn is often seen as the father of our solar system.

It takes Saturn almost thirty years to journey through the zodiac. So wherever he is placed in your chart he will return to in approximately thirty years. Many people see this 'Saturn return' as a very important time is one's life. It's a signifier of the end of youth and the beginning of midlife. This sometimes comes along with a midlife crisis and of course many people dread turning the big three-zero. As Saturn returns to his degree in your chart he brings many lessons. Any emotional or physical investments are rewarded and credit is given where credit is due. This can be negative or positive depending on the various seeds you've planted over the course of your life.

We see that Saturn's strict, father-like behavior is quite important in keeping the balance in our solar system, as well as the balance in our day to day lives. He creates boundaries and keeps our egos tamed. He shows us that patience is a virtue. And one of the most important influences he offers is the contemplation and reality of death. Our society sees this as negative but without death, there is no life.

Uranus

Day: Sunday / Number: 4 / Exalted in Scorpio

Uranus, Neptune and Pluto, are not used in ancient astrology since they could not be seen. When Uranus was discovered our solar system became much larger. Just the notion that there were planets beyond Saturn shook the foundation of astrological thought. This is Uranus's nature, to disrupt and to push boundaries. Uranus can be festering in the unconscious just waiting for the perfect moment to make a move, and when it does its dramatic and often can disrupt entire populations through social unrest and political influence. New technologies, new philosophy and new leadership are all governed by Uranus.

Uranus takes 84 years to complete its journey across the zodiac. This long journey often leads to him influencing entire generations during his travels. Entire cultures can be uprooted during a Uranus transit, especially if it's in a favorable sign that increases his influence.

Neptune

Day: Friday / Number: 6 / Exalted in Pisces

Neptune has a very fluid and watery behavior, but is much different than the moon. While the moon's watery behavior is super influential to our earthly lives in physical and emotional ways, Neptune has a more surreal watery attitude, governing the waters of our dreams and imaginations. Neptune dissolves boundaries and stimulates the imagination, offering big dreams and inspiration. Imagine deep caves in the oceans, or even the underworld itself. These are the lands of Neptune.

Neptune's influence can be quite disorienting if you're not prepared for his input. Hallucinatory at times, this energy can be confusing and often has symbolic interventions in our earthly lives. Your eyes and mind may play tricks on you, you may even feel as if you're in a dream. This elusive and mystical behavior can offer great insight into the mysteries of life and the dream realm, but you must be able to decipher the cryptic codes and understand the symbolism that manifests. If left unbalanced Neptune's influence can cause madness or seemingly insane thoughts. Drug use and escapism are common reactions to Neptune's intense energy, be wary of these habits during Neptune transits, but rest assured he moves slow, taking 165 years to travel the zodiac, so his is subtle for the most part.

Pluto

Pluto has had much controversy surrounding its label as a planet or not. There is also much debate in the astrological world about Pluto's influence. There is no ancient philosophy to base his influence on so more contemporary ideas are working out his influence.

If Pluto is accepted into the pantheon of astrological influence he is seen as a very under worldly influence. He moves very slowly across the zodiac so typically you will not see obvious influence from him in your personal life, he manifests on a generational scale, influencing entire generations depending on what sign he is in at the time. To follow his influence we look back at recent generations when he seems to make his existence known. Pluto is exalted in Leo.

Rahu & Ketu

In Vedic astrology before there were telescopes the north and south nodes of the moon were attributed to great influences on earth. These nodes are still used today, and often get associated with Neptune and Uranus numerology and attributes. These nodes are the exact spots where the moon's path and the sun's path intersect and are called Rahu and Ketu. Thus these nodes get a lot of sun and moon influence as well. Eclipses are associated with these nodes as well.

The image of a dragon is symbolic of these nodes, this image is powerful in many cultures and has been a great influence on astrological thinking, having associations with eclipses for millennia.

The north node, or Rahu, is seen as the dragon's head. This is where the node crosses the sun's path. Solar eclipses are a result of this node being conjunct to the sun or moon. Rahu deals in earthly experiences more than spiritual or subconscious ones.

The south node, or Ketu, is the dragon's tail. When the moon crosses the sun's path Ketu appears and teaches lessons of past lives and experiences into our consciousness. Ketu will also relieve you of emotional trauma and shock. Ketu deals mainly in spiritual or subconscious energies.

Rahu and Ketu do not rule any signs nor do they aspect other planets.

Astrology Basics

We will now explore in detail the basics of astrology. For whatever purpose you are planning to use astrology for this guide will be of great assistance. Take time to familiarize yourself with the concepts and vocabulary below.

Natal Charts

The position of the planets at the moment you were born is the basis of all personal astrology. Natal charts are a visual representation of this moment. This chart is comprised of a circular 360 degrees with twelve separate divisions of 30 degrees. These twelve divisions are the zodiac, with the most prominent constellations in the night sky within them. The celestial bodies within our solar system are then placed within this chart according to their position in the sky at the time of your birth. Imagine being in the town you were born in looking up at the sky at that moment. The planets and stars above the horizon comprise the upper half of your natal chart, whereas the planets below the horizon are the planets represented in the bottom half of your chart.

The constellations and planets move clockwise across the sky as it appears from earth. Of course we know that the solar system is not centered around the earth, but from our perspective the earth seems to be the center. This concept is important since our perception is essentially our basis of reality, what we experience is our lives. The constellations appear to move very slowly across the sky, and the planets are considered to be 'in' the constellations or 'signs'. The planets move at different speeds throughout these signs depending on their actual speed and distance from earth. These speeds also play into the behavior and attributes of that planet. For instance Mercury moves quite fast through the zodiac, taking as little as two weeks to pass through all twelve signs. Here mercury exhibits quick changing qualities, therefore this planet is attributed to swift communication and fast changing influences.

You can find your natal chart online by providing you date of birth, birth time and place of birth. It's helpful to be as exact as possible, if you do not know your birth time you will not be able to know your exact moon position and ascending signs can be affected. Otherwise the other planets are not greatly affected by being a few hours off. You need to provide the place you were born since the stars literally look different from different places on earth, especially in different hemispheres. This plays into the 'our perception is our reality' idea.

Once you have a copy of your natal chart you can study it and learn about your astrological makeup. For beginners it is recommended that you first memorize your sun sign, moon sign and ascendant. These three influences are the most noticeable and powerful energies, and need extra attention pertaining to the way they interact with other planets. Pay attention to where the planets are positioned throughout your day to day life as well. For instance most people already practice keeping track of their sun sign. When the sun returns to the exact degree as the one when you were born it's considered your birthday. Our contemporary calendar is a sun calendar, notice the 360 degrees of the zodiac versus 365 days. Therefore the sun takes 360-ish days to move through the zodiac. When a planet moves to the degree that it occupied in your natal chart it is called a transit. There are many aspects and transits happening consistently throughout your life, keeping track of these and preparing for their influence is core to the practice of astrology. You may also plan major events around these transits and aspects.

Houses

There are twelve divisions of an astrological chart that the signs and planets move within, these are called houses. The houses are representative of basic and broadly defined areas of life. These general areas of life are things everyone experiences and offer a simple overview of our existence, only once we analyze the planets or signs within the house does it get specific and distinct to our personal lives. These combinations are the basis of an astrological practice, so it is recommended that serious students memorize the houses and what each one represents.

The houses are ruled by certain planets and signs as well. This will be considered where the planet is most balanced and comfortable, not unlike a home. On the opposite end, there are also houses where certain planets are not 'at home' leaving their influence to be negative or weak. Let's look at each house in detail.

FIRST HOUSE

Ruled by Aries

This house governs your overall appearance, meaning how you physically appear as well as how you see yourself. Your impressions on others, how others look to you and overall how we carry ourselves in public are all attributed to the first house. This is often referred to as someone's 'vibe' or the energy they have when they enter a room. Your early childhood and surroundings are also found within this house.

SECOND HOUSE

Ruled by Taurus

This house governs wealth. This can certainly refer to financial wealth, but also mental and emotional wealth as well. Our ability to love, be compassionate and of course spend money wisely are greatly affected by this house and what planets are housed there. The friends and lovers we accumulate throughout life are indicative of this house, as well as religious beliefs or spirituality.

THIRD HOUSE

Ruled by Gemini

This house governs communication and interaction. Your internal dialogue and the way you speak to others is governed in this house. The way you text, write and move are indicative of what planets are housed here. Essentially any way you express yourself is dictated in the third house, so art, facial expressions, small talk and even the way you dress can be subtly influenced in this house.

FOURTH HOUSE

Ruled by Cancer

This house governs ancestry and roots. Your bloodlines and family affairs are housed here, as well as any future family plans. Whether or not you desire to have children is influenced in this house. Home life and the house you keep are touched by this house since they tie into procreation and raising children. Nurturing behaviors and relationships with your elders can be found here.

FIFTH HOUSE
Ruled by Leo

This house governs how you express yourself. Similar to communication, but focused more on a cultural aspects and how you react to things. Artistic endeavors and how your express love are found in this house. Emotional drama and conflicted emotions are common in the fifth house.

SIXTH HOUSE

Ruled by Virgo

This house governs your contribution to society. Whether or not you care about influencing others, or building community will be found in this house. Your ability to care about the environment or social political issues can be seen here, selflessness and selfishness are key factors in this house. How you care about yourself is found here as well, motivation to be healthy and active as well as mental clarity.

SEVENTH HOUSE

Ruled by Libra

This house governs relationships and connections with other people. These relationships are platonic and romantic, essentially any relationship you have with anyone is housed here. How you act within a friendship or romantic partnership is greatly affected by the planets and signs in this house. Promises, marriages, contractual agreements and other forms of commitment are found here.

EIGHTH HOUSE

Ruled by Scorpio

This house governs birth, sex and death. This transformative circle of life comprises some of the most important moments in someone's life. These milestones are often seen as taboo to talk about in many cultures but nonetheless they are very important to everyone's life. Intimate and mysterious, this house deserves special attention for understanding our lives. This house can also affect money and other material issues.

NINTH HOUSE

Ruled by Sagittarius

This house governs spirituality and spiritual progress. These higher states of experience are often ignored in our technological age of science, but still they play important roles in our existence. Cultural progress, religious experiences and adventures in other realms besides earth are governed in this house. Prejudice and moral problems can be helped by focusing on this house and the planets that reside within it.

TENTH HOUSE

Ruled by Capricorn

This house governs your public appearance and how you present yourself on the world stage. Big corporations and celebrities are immediate results of this house and its influence. Popularity and fame can be found in this house, as well as career choices outside of worldwide attention. This house gets a lot of attention since it affects our careers in such an important way. The cusp of this house is known as the midheaven, which tells a lot about someone's career paths. Many consult this area of the natal chart is they are having trouble finding what type of work they are meant to do in their life.

ELEVENTH HOUSE

Ruled by Aquarius

This house governs team building and how you get along with others. How you work in groups in school, groups at work and even religious groups can be found in this house. The 'team player' quality of people is influenced greatly by the sign and planet in this house. Loneliness, social acceptance, introverted and extroverted behavior are found here.

TWELFTH HOUSE

Ruled by Pisces

This house governs the completion of things. How you get stuff done and whether or not you are adept at finishing tasks are influenced in this house. Growing up, finding meaning in life and accepting time are great lessons to be learned in this house. This house can also affect death and the fear or acceptance that our lies will end. This 'full circle' idea is important to this house and the planets residing here will greatly affect how you come to terms with endings and letting go.

Vocabulary

Air Signs

Gemini, Libra and Aquarius are considered air signs. They govern intellect and deep thought.

Ascendant

The ascendant is more commonly known as the 'rising sign'. This sign is the constellation that is rising on the horizon the moment you are born. The influence of this sign is crucial in gaining insight into your 'mask' or how you present yourself to the world. Day to day socializing and defense mechanisms are greatly attributed to the ascendant sign

Aspects

When a planet creates a certain angle with another planet it is called an aspect. These angles create distinct relationships between the two or three planets in question. There are five major aspects in astrology; opposing, conjunct, sextile and square.

Configuration

Configurations are when there are aspects between three or more planets at one time.

Cusp

Dividing lines between the twelve signs are known as cusps. If a planet is about to change signs it is considered to be on the cusp of the two signs. Some astrologers believe this would give the planet influence form both signs, whereas just as many astrologers do not use cusps at all.

Decan

The decans are a treasure of Egyptian astrology, they divide up the 360 degrees of the zodiac into ten degree segments each with its own jurisdiction.

Degrees

The zodiac is comprised of 360 degrees, each planet moves a certain amount of degrees each day as it travels through the circle of signs. The sun moves one degree per day.

Descendant

The descendant is the opposite of the ascendant, so the sign that is descending into the horizon at the moment of your birth is your descendant.

Earth Signs

Taurus, Virgo and Capricorn are considered earth signs. They govern reason and practical thought.

Elements

The idea that everything is made up of elements is an ancient one. Earth, Air, Fire and Water are considered the four main elements. In astrology each planet has an elemental attribution, taking on the element's nature. For each element there are three signs assigned to it, each with a certain quality either fixed, mutable or cardinal.

Ephemeris

This is a word used in astrology to describe an astrological almanac. Typically these almanacs span one year of astrological timings and aspects.

Equinox

There are two days in the year when there are perfect amount of day and night. These are equinoxes, there is one in the spring and one in the autumn.

Fire Signs

Aries, Leo and Sagittarius are considered fire signs. They govern your temperament and passions.

Fixed Signs

Fixed signs have a stubborn and rooted behavior, the fixed signs are Taurus, Leo and Scorpio.

Grand Trine

When there are three planets that are trine to each other in the same elemental sign they are forming a Grand Trine.

Lilith

This planetary body is also known as the black moon, it is thought that there is an energy vortex or asteroid called Lilith that affects our astrology. The majority of astrological systems no longer use Lilith for readings.

Lunar Mansions

Lunar mansions can be seen almost as a lunar calendar. This calendar divides the zodiac into 27 or 28 divisions, these divisions are the lunar mansions and have their own influence of moon energy.

Mutable Signs

The mutable signs are generally open to change and fluxuations, they are Gemini, Virgo and Sagittarius,

Native

When someone is considered a native of a certain planet they are referring to the planetary ruler of their ascendant sign. For example if your ascendant is Aquarius then you are native to Saturn since it rules Aquarius.

Opposition

This is a type of aspect that is created when two planets are on opposite sides of the zodiac from each other, or 180 degrees apart.

Progressions

Progressions are used to forecast future events. You can see where the planets will be in the future and make plans or time events around the future configurations and aspects.

Qualities

Elemental qualities of a sign can be mutable, fixed or cardinal. These are the qualities of the sign.

Retrograde

At times planets can appear to move backwards in the sky, this means a planet is retrograde. This concentrates the planet's energy as it seems to swipe over the same area in a short amount of time.

Rulership

Certain planets rule certain signs, their energies are felt more intensely in sign that they rule.

Solstice

The days with the shortest amount of sunlight or longest amount of sunlight are known as solstices. The summer solstice is the longest day of the year and Winter solstice is the shortest day of the year.

Transit

A transit takes place when a planet moves through a sign or house. Planets can also transit your natal planets. For example Saturn can transit you natal Saturn as it moves through the sign and degree it was positioned at in your natal chart.

Void of Course

This term is typically referring to the moon, it describes the moon when it is creating no major aspects before it travels into a new sign. This can happen many times throughout a solar year.

Water

Cancer, Scorpio and Pisces are considered water signs. They govern emotional stability and intuitive thought.

CHAPTER 5
The Zodiac

Most of us are vaguely familiar with the zodiac, this twelve sign map of the heavens is used often in horoscopes and sun sign astrology. Horoscopes take the day you are born to find your sun sign then give a vague overview of how your week or month may go. These are not the most reliable astrological readings, but can be fun and a good way to learn a bit about your sun sign. But horoscopes don't take into consideration the other planet's positions when you're born, so they can't be relied upon for a serious reading.

The most prominent constellations in the sky make up the zodiac. The path that the sun takes through the sky is right through the middle of these signs, and the other planets travel through them on their own resected terms. The constellations themselves appear to move across the sky as well, but in the opposite direction as the planets. The constellations are as follows: Aries, Taurus, Gemini, Cancer, Leo, Virgo, Libra, Scorpio, Sagittarius, Capricorn, Aquarius and Pisces. All the planets move within these constellations.

When the studied we see distinct patterns as these plants dance through the sky. These patterns can be predicted decades in advance, even before technology our ancestors could predict events in the heavens, and thus how they affect our life on earth. The relationships between the planets and earth are very complicated, we cannot take full advantage of the astrological arts by only giving attention to the position of the sun in the zodiac.

The actual word zodiac is relatively new in western society it came to popularity in the 1970s along with the yoga astrology craze that flourished in America. The idea of the zodiac on the other hand is centuries old and an integral part of astrological practices today.

Signs

The twelve signs of the zodiac each have their own distinct influence upon the planets that are traveling through them. Combined with the energy of the planets themselves this influence can become quite complex as in makes its way into our lives on earth. Each sign is symbolically referred to using a sigil, animal image, color, stone and planetary ruler. These attributions are very well thought out and seek to make astrological practices simpler by giving the behavior of the heavens some earthly insights.

The influence we receive from these signs are very important to astrology itself. While the planets are greatly influential on their own, but without the context of a sign to organize the energy the planets would be imparting an intensely erratic energy. The signs offer broad insight into our personal lives and futures, while the planets affect more subtle energies and are focused heavily in the present moment.

The signs all have their own attributes and behaviors that are distinct to them. While the signs to work together through the planets as they aspect each other across the zodiac, they are largely regarded as single influences, many parts creating the whole. Let's look at the signs in more detail to get to know them better.

Aries

Symbol: Ram / Element: Cardinal Fire / Ruled by Mars

As far as the astrological months are concerned Aries is the first month, this is due to the spring equinox which would be the start of the sun in Aries and the beginning of longer days. This is fitting for Aries and its fiery nature. The fiery and stoic nature of Aries is also very fitting for its ram symbol. Courageous and full of life, Aries loves a good competition and prefers to win. Your leadership qualities and ability to give orders is influenced greatly by Aries.

Being able to solve problems efficiently and in a fair way is another Aries influence. This quality allows the proud Aries to balance out his self-involved nature by being fair as well as full of pride. Natives to the Aries influence may be overly excited and impatient, as well as warm and welcoming. Aries is very competitive but will only feel rewarded from their success if they win fairly. Aries may be easily upset but they never stay mad for too long.

Taurus

Symbol: Bull / Element: Fixed earth / Ruled by Venus

The energy of Taurus is relatively balanced. Patience and peacefulness are the norm for this sign, but if excited Taurus energy can be very disruptive. Enjoyment of the arts and music is a must for Taurus. These natives prefer to be comfortable and enjoy food and libation slowly. This comfort must be accompanied by stability or the Taurus native may become agitated or stressed.

Taurus anger is notorious in the astrological sphere, if Taurus manages to become upset they go full force in their reactions, often being demanding or rude. Taurus prefers to follow rules rather than taking short cuts or cheating, this honorable quality pairs well with his stoicism and reliability. People with a heavy Taurus influence often are indecisive, but this is no trouble for the relaxed nature as long as it doesn't cause financial losses.

Gemini

Symbol: Twins / Element: Mutable Air / Ruled by Mercury

The influence of Gemini offers many skills predominantly in writing or teaching. The symbol of the twins is indicative of the sign's love of sharing and teamwork. These team player qualities add a great skill in communication as well. Gemini is genuinely curious about other's interests and life paths. They can have a conversation about any topic, and love to learn new things.

Gemini is not a fan of being alone, they tend to rely on others for fun and success. This is troublesome for Gemini natives who can often be too reliant on others, seeking social situations too often and not taking time to learn about themselves. The Gemini energy is very social, they get along with all types of people and love to travel to exotic places.

Cancer

Symbol: Crab / Element: Cardinal Water / Ruled by the moon

The symbol of the crab is very fitting for the energy of Cancer. They tend to be homely in any situation and hold on tightly to things they desire. They are prone to erratic moving and stubborn ideas about what is correct behavior. This can be beneficial and negative for the Cancer native, unless they have a foundation or family anchoring them down, they tend to run from problems rather than tending to them.

While avoiding unnecessary confrontation, Cancers do well with family affairs and relationships as long as they are in control. They fear losing family the most of any fear, and tend to be possessive and demanding. This passivity often gets mistaken for carelessness, but in fact they are very caring. Cancer's influence can offer insight into spiritual affairs, as long as there isn't anything stressful blocking their vision.

Leo

Symbol: Lion / Element: Fixed Fire / Ruled by Sun

The energy of Leo is energetic and full of pride. Dignified and confident, Leo natives love being the center of attention and performing for crowds. We see here that the lion is a perfect symbol for the Leo's behavior. Leo influence can sometimes be narcissistic and self-involved, leading one to believe that they have all the answers. This overconfidence can be troublesome at times, it is an important lesson to the Leo native to balance this behavior. For leadership roles Leo energy fits very well as long as they don't take advantage of their powerful role.

Le is always looking at the big picture. Little mundane details and tasks that have no immediate reward are of no concern to Leo, he is focused on huge problems and big solutions. While Leo seems like he's in control he often ensures that others are seeing his success, and that they approve. If he doesn't get immediate approval he may be defensive, not willing to admit he was wrong. This is common of the Leo energy, but even if they won't say it aloud, they do learn from their mistakes.

Virgo

Symbol: Maiden / Element: Mutable Earth / Ruled by Mercury

Virgo energy is clear headed and has a great ability to stay focused. This one pointed nature comes in handy in all parts of life. Virgo will listen quietly to all the details before speaking up with their personal opinions. This can be detrimental if the Virgo native is too passive, but this is easily resolved as they do wish their voices to be heard.

Crafts and quiet creative endeavors are perfect for Virgo natives, they appreciate a quiet evening of contemplation or meditation. Virgo influence will cause one to spend their time wisely, making sure they have their errands and other mandatory tasks completed before rest and relaxation. Virgo may be quiet and reserved but she must contribute to society in positive ways, if even a small amount. This selflessness and patient sign loves working with the underprivileged and minorities.

Libra

Symbol: Scales / Element: Cardinal Air / Ruled by Venus

The set of scales is a suitable symbol for the sign of Libra. Balance is the key to Libra's influence as it tries to create this balance in everything it can reach. This natural ability to create balance comes in handy for any walk of life. Even if the balance cannot be created in the present moment, Libra energy offers the foresight to see how an unbalanced situation may lead to balance in the future. Naturally this balance allows Libra to make smart decisions, they quickly weigh the option and potential circumstances then act.

The desire for harmony makes Libra natives delightful to have around, they often are willing to sacrifice their own desires to balance out a scenario. This energy also influences one to be empathetic to their loved ones, often seeing a positive side to a negative situation. Beware though this behavior can have a reverse effect if the native is looking only to the negative side of things. This pessimism is easy to get lost in and can push loved ones away.

Scorpio

Symbol: Scorpion / Element: Fixed Water / Ruled by Pluto

The energy of Scorpio is typically serious and introspective. Adequate time to think things through is needed for Scorpio to make important decisions. This patience and attention to detail is favorable in most situations, but if channeled into a negative way can cause serious harm. You do not want to be an enemy of a person with heavy Scorpio influence in their chart. This tendency toward deep thought can make some people over analytical or obsessive.

Many Scorpio natives are quiet and reserved, but this is only at first to give them time to size you up. They are a good judge of character and can make friends with almost anyone, often with ulterior motives. It is tough to deceive a Scorpio, they are very observant and tend to have a firm grip on their surroundings. Rarely frightened or intimidated, Scorpios will not hesitate to stand up for what they believe in. They also love to be challenged throughout their life.

Sagittarius

Symbol: Centaur / Element: Mutable Fire / Ruled by Jupiter

This optimistic sign influences people to let loose and be spontaneous. Adventures and exciting activities are needed to keep the attention of these natives, they tend to wander or get bored. Not unlike the mythological centaur, this influence inspires one to roam or make decisions on a whim, seeking new experiences. Nomadic mindset and living well under their means are very Sagittarian qualities.

If the Sagittarius is not able to roam free or do as they please they can get depressed or feel unfulfilled. Sagittarius truly thrives on the unexpected and open ended nature of adventure. This can cause people to not finish important projects or leave long term goals alone. Culture and sports are favorites of these natives they love to play and despise prejudice.

Capricorn

Symbol: Goat / Element: Cardinal Earth / Ruled by Saturn

Capricorn is a sign of logical thought and structured action. This energy inspires a strong work ethic and logical attention to material gain. Capricorn loves to know what's going to happen next and tends to over plan, only to be disappointed as their overly distinct plans do come through. They appreciate routines and must have a project in progress to feel fulfilled.

These natives are skilled in many talents, and they put meticulous effort into their work. Careers that are stressful or challenging are perfect for Capricorn influences, often people need intense outlets for this strong energy. The Capricorn native is also very strict about fairness and justice. They tend to be diplomatic and are always on the defensive, which sometimes causes trouble with loved ones. As the voice of reason in most situations, they tend to not be spontaneous or adventurous.

Aquarius

Symbol: Water Bearer/ Element: Fixed Air / Ruled by Uranus

This sign offers very nurturing and caring influences, often inspiring people to start families or volunteer. Aquarius natives will happily offer their help or resources to assist those in need. This selfless nature is constant in the mind of Aquarius, sometimes this can detrimental if the person does not cater to their personal emotional needs. They can also be taken advantage of if they are being too passive or selfless.

Along with this sense of humility, Aquarius is clever and thoughtful. They are fun to be around and love planning social events. Their empathy and dedication makes them great for the service industry or work in hospitals. They do not pass judgement on others, but may be hard on themselves over little mistakes or discrepancies. Gardens and caring for farms are common lifestyles for the water bearer.

Pisces
Symbol: Fish / Element: Mutable Water / Ruled by Neptune

Pisces offers an influence that is graceful and discreet, they can move swiftly through fulfilling lives without recognition or fame. They value rhythm and routine and prefer to have plenty of personal space. Although shy and quiet, there is usually strong emotions running through the Pisces native's mind, being easily inspired by art, nature and technology. Pisces love keeping secrets and can be trusted with the most important tasks.

Pisces is in no rush to prove their self-worth, they know who they are and would rather not boast about their successes. Although very intelligent and creative Pisces may keep their insight to themselves. People are often surprised when their quiet Pisces friends spout a quick joke or cunning wisdom, these small insights into their minds are enlightening. If Pisces natives are able to get out of their heads they can do great things with their natural knack for spiritual arts and imaginative perspectives.

CHAPTER 6
Personal Astrology

We see that astrology is much more complex than just looking up your sun sign in the back of the newspaper. There are as many combinations and variable as there are human emotions and experiences. The obvious energies can be easily felt, while the more subtle ones need some extra attention. Now that you have a little experience and hopefully your sun, moon and ascendant sign memorized, we can dig a little deeper into how to use this information in your practice.

Skills in astrology are limitless, this art can be practiced for a lifetime and the student will still only scratch the surface. Seeing into the future, timing events perfectly and improving our understanding of existence are great feats that can be accomplished through this art, but what about our general health? With astrology you tend to be organized in day to day life once you start your practice. You know when drama is coming so you save time by avoiding it. You choose suitable days to run errands and avoid car trouble or forgetting important tasks. You know when to expect troubling times and can prepare. Any of these benefits is going to relieve stress, which in turn will lead a healthier life.

There are many theories as to how astrology works. At the very least it's a powerful calendar and contextual symbolic exercise for your mind. At its most influential the plants are actually having physical and spiritual effects on the earth. More spiritual models believe that the entities that thrive on these planets can be reached and used to help on earth. Whatever you believe is up to you, but be sure that your beliefs fit in with what you have experienced. And of course, if it works, then it works, it doesn't really matter why or how. Whether you are trying to reach spirits to commune with, or just seeking some psychological analysis, astrology can help.

Technology can help us keep track of our personal astrology. Find an app that keeps your natal chart handy. Or use the available technology to map the skies at night. It is only reasonable to use this technology to our advantage. The art of astrology is ancient so must be approached with humility, and this can be done with modern technology, but if you are able to practice without the intensive intervention of screens or phones then it will be that much more effective. The more effort you put in, the more you will get out.

Let's get into detail about some ways to use technology to our advantage. These techniques are perfect for beginners and will help you successfully begin to rebuild your relationship with the heavens.

Personal Signs

As we mentioned in earlier chapters, the sun sign, moon sign and ascendant are the most influential energies and a perfect three to start out with. These three influences impact you directly but also relate to the other influences in very important ways. The sun being a foundational energy source. The moon being a mirror and emotional dictator. And the ascendant being your mask and social defense mechanism. These three influences will greatly affect how the other planet's energies interact with you, almost needing these three main influences to manifest on earth in an organized way.

Below we will discuss these three main influences in detail, as well as how other planets can be used to navigate our lives on earth.

Sun Sign

The sun sign is the most common referred to sign in astrology. Typically when people refer to themselves as a certain sign they are referring to their sun sign. The sun sign is constellation that the sun is in at the time of your birth. This sign will be the most influential to your foundation and source of inspiration. Almost like a battery the sun energizes this sign and it moves through you consistently throughout your life, almost filtering other influences through itself.

Our society's most widely used calendar is a sun sign calendar so it's much easier to keep track of. Here are the signs and dates the sun resides within them;

Aries: March 21 – April 19

Taurus: April 20 – May 20

Gemini: May 21 – June 20

Cancer: June 21 – July 22

Leo: July 23 - August 22

Virgo: August 23 - September 22

Libra: September 23 - October 22

Scorpio: October 23 - November 21

Sagittarius: November 22 - December 21

Capricorn: December 22 - January 19

Aquarius: January 20 - February 18

Pisces: February 19 - March 20

Your birthdate with tell you your sun sign in the above chart if you do not know it. Take note of your sun sign and learn its behaviors. Do you see similarities in your life and the sign's attributes? Can you relate to its behaviors? This sign will be the most consistently influential energy throughout your life, get to know it well, it is the foundation of your astrological make up.

Moon Sign

The moon sign is a little bit more difficult to keep track of than the sun sign. You will need to know the exact time you were born to have an accurate moon sign calculation. The moon moves so quickly through the signs that she often moves into a new sign during a solar day. By using technology or an ephemeris we can find out where the moon was positioned when we were born. Once you know this sign keep note of its relation to the sun sign and how these signs interact with the moon's behavior.

It is suggested that astrology students follow the moon closely. No other planet is responsible for such obvious influence on earth than the moon. Emotional uproars, strange energy in the air and odd behavior are common outcomes from the moon's placement. By keeping track of her you can better navigate her influence. The moon goes through all the signs of the zodiac in almost 29 days, this means she is changing signs every two to three days. If you memorize the order of the signs you can find out what sign the moon is currently in and keep track of her travels.

The moon cycles are important as well. Depending on how full the moon is, or whether she is waning or waxing she has different behaviors. This fluidity and change of behavior makes the moon a very finicky energy to work with, but you can form a respectful relationship with her to ease her negative influence and enjoy her positive influence. Many cultures in the past have adhered to a lunar calendar. Many festivals and feasts are planned for full moons, not to mention the association with witchcraft and other magical practices.

Ascendant

We have mentioned that the ascendant is the sign that is rising on the horizon at the time of your birth. If you could imagine the horizon the sign would be on the far left hand side rising up in a clockwise motion. You will need a natal chart to figure out what you rising sign is.

Other Planets

You can find out where the other planets were positioned by going online or using an app to get your natal chart. This chart can be found online on many sites. You are not expected to memorize all the positions and aspects but if you feel a certain attraction to any certain planet it is wise to study its influence in your chart. Once you have a full grasp of the main three influences, move your way through all the planets and their energies. Be aware of transits and natal returns, these times are often very intense for better or for worse.

As you track your planets as they aspect each other throughout the year, you can take actions to work with these planets. Many traditions involve planetary prayers and offerings to spirits of these planets. Not unlike the worship of Greek gods, the planets and their influence can be treated like a relationship. You pray and give offerings to let the planets know you are humble in your approach to them. They may shine more favorable energies upon you if you are in good grace with them. These are magical techniques that aim to empower the individual, if you go this route you should take great care in your practices, be humble and be dedicated.

Aspects

Let's now talk about the major aspects that planets make with each other. In astrology it is thought that when two or more planets create angles in the zodiac that they are working together in powerful ways to combine influences. These aspects are created when two or more planets are a certain number of degrees from each other. The aspects that are most powerful are considered hard aspects, while the other aspects are less noticeable and are called soft aspects.

In a broad sense the planets are always working with each other regardless of placement in the zodiac, but these aspects greatly intensify the effects. Each aspect offers its own twist on influences as well. Having hard aspects in a natal chart give very distinct personality traits, these aspects should be paid close attention to for the beginner in astrology.

Let's learn more of the details about these prominent aspects and how they affect the planets and their influences.

Conjunct Aspects

When two or more planets are in conjunction they are within a few degrees of each other. Many astrologers adhere to the rule that two planets need to be within ten degrees of each other to be conjunct. This aspect is thought to be one of the more powerful aspects that can take place.

When planets are conjunct they tend to work harmoniously together. Although this isn't always the case, for instance if the planets are conjunct but in an unfavorable sign or forming aspects with your natal planets in an unfavorable way.

When three or more planets are conjunct it is called a stellium, this creates a very intense energy that may be tough to navigate. The variety of influence may also make it tough to tell which planet is causing what effect.

Sextile Aspect

When two or more planets are 60 degrees apart from each other they create a sextile aspect. This aspect influences the planets to be creative and work together in unexpected or disruptive ways. Although the planets will be working together well, it may still be disruptive in your personal life. This aspect adds a dynamic effect and allows the planets to mesh together in interesting ways that aren't otherwise found with other aspects. Sextile aspects are related to the 3rd and 11th houses.

Square Aspect

When two or more planets are 90 degrees from each other they create a square aspect. For square aspects it is thought that outer planets influence the inner planets more so and not vice versa. Square aspects are notorious for troublesome or complex influences. Drama may ensue or some mundane inconvenience may arise during these aspects. Square aspects are related to eh 4th and 10th houses.

Trine Aspect

Trine aspects are formed when two or more planets are 120 degrees from each other. This brings in a 'power of three' influence, which offers progressive and forward thinking energy. This can come about harmoniously or through disruption, although typically ends well even if it's through disruption. Hidden desires and skills come to fruition, secrets are revealed and pleasant surprises may arise with this aspect. Conflicts often get resolved during these aspects. Trine aspects relate to the 5th and 9th houses.

Opposition Aspect

When two or more planets are 180 degrees apart they are creating an opposition aspect. These planets will be directly across a chart from each other. This aspect almost always causes a conflicting energy, often bringing tension and added stressors. The planets may be butting heads or struggling to mesh well during these times, creating similar effects on earth. While this is seen as negative most of the time, opposites may attract for a reason and the end result may be worthwhile. Opposition aspects may teach valuable lessons if you are able to see through the troubles it caused. Opposition aspects are related to the 7th house.

Minor Aspects

The major aspects above are the most commonly used in astrology. While there are many other aspects happening almost always, the major ones tend to be the most notable and obvious. Some astrologers don't work with minor aspects but it's still good to give them a mention for our intentions with this book.

The following is a list of the most common minor aspects:

Semi-sextile – 30 degrees apart

Quintile – 72 degrees apart

Septile – 51 degrees apart

Semi-square – 45 degrees apart

As mentioned above, the planets are always working together to influence the events on earth. But we see with aspects that their relationships to each other reach highs and lows, while forming aspects that concentrate their energies in various ways. This all may seem complex, but just a little time to learn these common phrases and configurations will go a long way in developing your personal practice. Let's dive even deeper into our astrological realm with planetary hours.

Planetary Hours

We have seen that each day has a planetary ruler, Sunday=Sun ruler, but even deeper and more subtle energy comes from the planetary ruler of a certain hour of the day. This adds to the complexity of astrology but is crucial for favorable timing on a whim, if you know the planetary ruler of the hour, you will be better prepared for the spontaneous influences that arise in the hour.

For instance if it's Tuesday, day of Mars, and you're approaching a Mars ruled hour, it may be smart to prepare for a mild conflict or assertive feelings. Even more so if Mars is in a Mars ruled sign, or you have a Mars transit taking place. The use of planetary hours only affects the seven classical planets in astrology, so Neptune, Uranus and Pluto are left out of this concept. This is due to the use of planetary hours predating telescopes, way back to Babylon. Here is where we get the name for the order of planets as well, the Chaldean order.

The Chaldean order was made by arranging the slowest to fastest planets from earth's perspective. So as they appear on earth, whichever planet takes the longest to complete it zodiac journey from earth's perspective will be placed first on the list. To determine the planetary hour we need to take this order into consideration.

To find the planetary hour of any given day is pretty complicated without an app or website but it can be done. Depending on what day it is the first hour of the day pertains to that specific day. So the first hour of the day for Saturday is ruled by Saturn. We need to keep in mind that in this system the first hour of the day begins as the sun rises in the morning, not at midnight like our current timing system. Once we have the hourly ruler we take the order of the week and look three days previous to know which planet rules the next hour.

For example if we are in the first hour of Saturn on Saturday, then we would count three days previous; Saturday, Friday, Thursday. Jupiter rules the next hour since Jupiter rules Thursday. Count three previous to Thursday and you will get the next hour's ruler; Thursday, Wednesday, Tuesday. Mars rules the next hour since Mars rules Tuesday. This can be done in this pattern over and over, eventually you get back to Saturn around midday, and then to Saturn again just before nightfall.

We see here that the order of planetary rulers for the hours goes in the following pattern for Saturday: Saturn, Jupiter, Mars, Sun, Venus, Mercury, Moon then back to Saturn. This pattern can be applied to any day with the respected ruler of the day beginning the list. This follows with our Gregorian calendar to start the new day with the proper ruler of the day for our well-known order of Sunday, Monday, Tuesday, Wednesday, Thursday, Friday and Saturday.

Planetary hours may seem complicated, but with an app to keep track of these rulers you can easily know what hour it is at any given time. Using the hourly rulers is great for timing things spontaneously on any given day, as well as planning your days accordingly. If a certain planet is already having a heavy influence on your natal chart or current chart and it's their day to rule, and they are ruling the current hour you will have a very intensive concentration of the planet's energy.

Practice

When you are ready to openly start working with the planets and their energies, there are many different ways to go about the practice. While timing and planning is relatively simple to practice, you're more so navigating through and around the influences of the planets. There are ways to directly embrace the planet's energies as well, these techniques are found in many magical systems and other spiritual systems that believe the planets have intelligences or spirits that interfere on earth. The point of these practices would be to humbly welcome or invite the energy into your life. These techniques will increase the influence of planets exponentially, be cautious when approaching these energies in this manner, and as always be respectful and humble.

Prayer

Many people find prayer to be unattractive due to its connotations to religions and popular spiritual models. In astrology you do not use prayer to ask the planets for anything for yourself, but you are better off praying that you hope their endeavors are successful. For instance instead of praying for a certain thing, you would pray that the planet has great success in all their endeavors and then welcome the planet's influence into your life.

There are many prayers found in ancient texts and spiritual books, but composing your own is just as effective. Write down a set of prayers that pertain to each planet, thanking them and complimenting them. Make it poetic and flowing, preferably easy to remember. These words are well-suited to communing with the planets. Songs, poems and other rhythmic words work very well.

Many ancient prayers involve naming god and other intelligences, if this isn't something you prefer to do you may leave out any reference to god and focus on the planets.

Timing

We have touched on timing a little bit in previous chapters, but there are many different timing techniques. Whether you're timing a small errand or planning a big event like a wedding, these timings are only to help ensure success in the desired plan. Planning a long road trip is not recommended if Mercury is placed unfavorably or retrograde since he governs travel. These little nuances will help you save time and effort if planned accordingly.

When deciding what would be a good time to plan something there are many variables to take into consideration. While the current astrological chart is important, you need to take into consideration your natal chart as well as anyone else's natal placements. You should also consider your numerology as well. For instance, if it's a wedding you're planning you would want to look at the natal charts of the bride and groom, see where there are any discrepancies and pick a day where these less-than-favorable placements may be a problem. If the groom has an unfavorable placement of Venus, then pick a day when Venus is exalted or balanced, a Friday in the hour of Venus would be ideal. Or even Venus in Taurus on a Friday would be more Venusian influence.

There are almost limitless ways to arrange and rearrange these timings. Be sure to take meticulous attention when deciding on these plans and events. Sometimes things pop up unexpectedly so you may not have time to plan it according to the astrology, this is where having a nice prayer memorized comes into play, and you could quickly grab a certain planet's attention if an unexpected event arises.

Offerings

Leaving offerings or gifts for gods and long lost ancestors is still popular in our culture today. We leave flowers on graves and even poor out drinks for lost friends. But this same form of respect can be used to get the attention of the planets and gain their favor. Our ancient ancestors would leave offerings and prayers for the spirits to appease their unfavorable behavior. This practice is great to help build relationships with the planets.

Many people use an altar to leave offerings and perform their magical routines. This is not necessary but works great if you have limited space or want to really have a nice space for your practice. Altars can be made of almost anything, but the more effort you put forth the better. If you do not want an altar you can leave offerings outdoors near a favorite tree or near a body of water.

For the actual offerings themselves you want to choose something associated with the planet in question. Water, incense and money are easy go-to gifts that are universal for most planets, but it's recommended to leave something specific to the plane as well. For instance for Venus leave beautiful flowers or a candle of the suitable color. Jupiter loves money and the color purple. Alcohol also makes a great universal offering, poor out your first drink of the day anytime you're indulging. It's safe to say that the more valuable something is to you the more interested the planets will be in it. Water is a good offering, but go buy spring water, or soak herbs in the water beforehand.

With the practice of offerings we can even combine prayer and timing. Let's say it's Saturday and you want to have a nice meditative session at your altar. To exalt the experience you would wait for the hour of Saturn on Saturday to perform this ritual. Have your altar and surrounding area clean. Light a black candle and incense, say a prayer for Saturn then leave your chosen offerings. If you have the time you may want to set quietly as you see and feel if Saturn energy is more prominent in this moment.

Many recommend that your do not try and work with multiple planets at once, ease yourself into the practice and pay close attention to the different effects that take place after you begin this practice. This is considered astrological magic and is taken very seriously in spiritual communities.

The use of these astrological practices above is in no way the extent of every technique. The methods listed above are good for beginners, but also play into our purpose for this book. Numerology, Tarot and Astrology all can be worked together to optimize desired results. We chose offerings, timing and prayer because they will sync up well with a numerology or tarot practice. Keep these techniques in mind as we move on to the next chapter.

CHAPTER 7
Tarot

Mysterious and inviting, tarot cards have been used for millennia to predict future events or gain insight into the true nature of reality. These cards come in many forms but typically are adorned with beautiful artwork that invokes complex thought and invite the practitioner to sort through the deck almost as if they are under a spell. The art of predicting future events is called divination. Predictive astrology techniques are considered divination as well, but the tarot are the most widely used and popular means of practicing this art.

The traditional deck of 52 playing cards are even find their history rooted in the tarot. The numbers, images and esoteric meanings found within are still powerful even with a mass produced deck. It's unknown how cards can hold or promote such power, but it is very real and has been used by our ancient ancestors to learn the secrets of existence. Today we see tarot everywhere, card game are ever popular and themed tarot decks can be found at tourist gift shops all around the world. Even with popular culture capitalizing on the art tarot remains powerful and effective for communion with the subtle forces of nature.

There are literally thousands of tarot decks available, from traditional occult decks to decks with images of puppies or dragons. Regardless of the tarot theme these decks can be powerful. It brings up the question of whether it's the deck that holds power or does the deck just act as a catalyst for human's potential to contact unseen forces. Whatever tarot deck you find, we will reiterate that if it works, then it works.

What is Tarot?

As we mentioned, there are thousands of tarot decks all around the planet. Some are creatively designed and instilled with occult energy and images. Others seem to just cater to niche demographics, with teddy bears or zoo animals printed on them. For our book here we will focus on the spiritual nature of these cards, rather than just aesthetically pleasing ones.

It's been said that if someone were to be sheltered from the world and knew nothing about life, they could be given a tarot deck and learn the secrets to life with just the deck itself. This is a bold claim but it aims mainly to get the point across that these cards are powerful beyond random images that our brains seek meaning within. This being said, one cannot just buy a deck and learn to use them instantly. It takes years to learn to listen to these cards, working with them requires patience and an open heart.

Many seek the tarot to answer tough questions about love and life, their personal lives being the key interest. Other people use these cars to commune with spirits and communicate with the unseen realms, the insights found here are beyond our earthly love lives. Whatever approach you take to the tarot, keep in mind that you don't need to study extensively into the 'meanings' of the cards. Simply read them and listen if anything comes through, there is no one way that works for everyone.

Tarot deck s can contain many different images as well as structures. The standard deck contains 78 cards divided into two groups, the major arcana and the minor arcana. These groups have different intentions and insights, this structure is the style that all other decks are compared to. Some people have invented decks with more or less cards, and some may only use half of standard deck, it all depends on what feels right to them. Keep this open mindedness with you as you approach the tarot.

Minor Arcana

The minor arcana is comprised of 56 cards, these cards are divided into four suits, just like the contemporary playing cards we have today. These suits are quite similar to the standard playing card decks as well, they are as follows; Coins, batons, swords and cups.

In magical circles these suits can be altered slightly to be pentacles, wands, swords and cups respectively.

Each of these four suits has ten numbered cards and four court cards. Similar to playing cards the court cards are not numbered and are comprised of kings, queens, knights, and pages. These 56 cards more closely resemble playing cards used in games like poker today, but the Major Arcana is a world of its own.

Major Arcana

The major arcana is also referred to as the trump cards. This group is comprised of 22 numbered card with no suits. They are much more open to interpretation than the minor arcana since the suits in the minor arcana offer some sort of context to think with. With the major arcana each card has an image that is complex and carries a story within it. These can be interpreted many different ways, but many tarot readers adhere to a loose structure of meanings and correspondences.

0. Fool
I. Magician
II. High Priestess
III. Empress
IV. Emperor
V. Hierophant
VI. Lovers
VII. Chariot
VIII. Strength
IX. Hermit
X. Wheel of Fortune
XI. Justice
XII. Hanged Man
XIII. Death
XIV. Temperance
XV. Devil
XVI. Tower
XVII. Star

XVIII. Moon
  XIX. Sun
   XX. Judgement
  XXI. World

This list may just seem like a jumble of random words, but once you see them you can see slight relations and meanings, almost as if the cards tell a story in order. Although when working with the cards they will not likely be in any particular order.

The Cards

We find that the tarot is just as complex as astrology and numerology. This is to be expected with any occult art form. Before we learn how to work with the cards we can take a look at some vague meanings that are attributed to the cards. These meanings are in no way set in stone, but work as a broad guide to the cards.

We will begin with the minor arcana and make our way all the way through to the major arcana.

Wands / Batons

Ace – this card represents the start of an action. Creation and invention are key characteristics of this card. Origins and ancestry come into play and new beginnings are common. Money and fortune can be an attribute of this card.

Two – Dominion and rulership are key to this card. Completing projects and taking the lead to get something done correctly. This card may signify that you need to take action or control of a situation.

Three – This card signifies movement and impulsive action. This could mean moving onto a new chapter in life or something smaller like a new creative project. New business opportunities and creative endeavors may be in the near future.

Four – Completion is key to this card. Wrapping up unfinished projects or tying loose ends are recommended by this card. Conclusions and fulfillment of prophecy may be in the coming days.

Five – Conflict and adversity are associated with this card. This may mean that hard work needs to be done soon or that an enemy may arise. Preparation is needed to combat these coming changes.

Six – This card may signify victory over an enemy or adverse scenario. It may also mean that there is superiority or one-sidedness in a certain scenario. This may mean that your actions are being tested or judged.

Seven – Bravery and stoicism come along with this card. This could mean bravery in the face of danger or even being brave to embrace changes or discoveries. You may see actions rewarded or punished.

Eight – This card brings along quickness, whether it's physical quickness or mental quickness. Improvisation and clear thinking may be needed soon.

Nine – This card signifies health and strength. These qualities are not fleeting or should they be abandoned. Any negative or self-deprecating thoughts may be extinguished.

Ten – This card is considered to be representative of oppression. You or someone you know may be oppressed or the oppressor. This could bring heavy responsibilities, troubles or a sense of being out of control.

King – Honesty and a mysterious seriousness comes with this card. Important decisions may need your input or expertise. It may be your duty to uplift or reassure.

Queen – This card may similar to the king of wands, but less mysterious and more welcoming. This card may signify fertility or good harvest as well.

Knight – This card could signify change of environment or a long mysterious adventure. This may bring loneliness or a sense of individualism.

Page – Dedication and favorable relationships come with this card. This may mean success in friendship or love, but generally a successful search for meaning.

Cups

Ace – this card represents the birth of emotions. There is potential for creative endeavors, strengthening of loving relationships and emotional progress.

Two – This card brings balance to relationships. Comfort and contented feelings are abundant. The relationships you have built are calm and drama free, or may be sooner than later.

Three – This card signifies loving abundance. Marriages or engagements are in store. There may be a pregnancy or rebirth of an old relationship. Any loving union may be yielding a new era or gift.

Four – Indulgent living and maximum enjoyment are present. You may be overindulging or at risk of exhaustion if not kept in check. Luxuries and unnecessary gifts are a plenty.

Five – This card is often associated with failing or being defeated. Frustrations and inadequacy are present.

Six – This card signifies a state of pleasure. Sensual stimulation and balanced feasts may be in store. Enjoyment of the highest levels can be found and leasing music or other art is in the near future.

Seven – Corruption due to sensual pleasures and indulgences are abound. This may in efforts to lead you away from your responsibilities or jobs that need to be finished soon.

Eight – This card may signify laziness or procrastination. Slow moving ideas and lack of motivation.

Nine – This card is balanced and pleasurable. It incites happiness to come and calm waters ahead. Everything will be balanced soon or already is in progress. A very favorable card for most readings.

Ten – Happiness and balance may need some tending to, you realize this takes a lot of work to maintain. Keeping the balance will require great strides and patient attitudes.

King – Feelings of elderly wisdom, but may take some effort to decipher. Dreams and mysteries affect day to day living.

Queen – Passivity and daydreaming, this card may signify the letting down of defense mechanisms and walls. Your inspirations and influences are exposed.

Knight – This card has a secretive nature, seeming calm but experiencing intense passions consistently. This closed off nature leads to distrust and conspicuous attitudes.

Page – Thankful and sweet, romanticism may arise in the near future. Beauty is plentiful and found in all aspects of life, a sense of wonder and carelessness is prominent.

Swords

Ace – Your sense of identity and personal opinions are growing. This birth of individual ideas and opinions can be misleading to outsiders but beneficial to you and your growth.

Two – Peaceful and harmonious exists between individuals or nations. Tranquil and calm this card ushers in understanding and resolved conflicts. This may be in relationships or within an individual.

Three – Sadness and grief may be in store. There may be disappointments or unlucky circumstances in the near future. Conflicts do not get resolved and may manifest in the coming days.

Four – this card signifies a stalemate or tie. This may be a reconciliation of differences, regardless of the state of hostility, there is a break or resolution, but the damage is very much done so it's time to attend to the damages.

Five – This card is very straightforward and represents defeat. This may be you defeating or being defeated, but something is coming to an abrupt ending. This may be a big fight or small discrepancy.

Six – Rational knowledge and scientific facts are needed. It's time to apply what you know for sure to your life and put you knowledge into action. Enrolling in school, major studies and insightful travel may be in store.

Seven – Feelings of uselessness and inequality may arise. This card represents a lack of meaning and confusion about life. Even inspiring events are being questioned and questioned for their validity.

Eight – This card typically represents interference and disruption. Miscommunications and misunderstandings arise, causing detrimental effects on the physical and mental faculties.

Nine – This card is indicative of cruelty, whether it's unfair trials, rude behavior or physical harm. All things cruel are potentially on the horizon. This may manifest in divorce, physical fights or abuse of power.

Ten – This card can represent ruins or destruction. Demolition of old buildings or destruction of old habits are abound. This can be positive or negative destruction but destruction nonetheless.

King – Professionalism and attention to detail. Careers may improve and work may be abundant. Professional appearance and demeanor are commonplace, they should be paid close attention to.

Queen – Losing a loved one or romantic partner may be in the future. This card represents widows, lonely women and the saddened individual who has recently experienced a great loss.

Knight – An aspirational card, this one may represent ideals and political ideas that are powerful and attainable. Deception may arise from this and social upheaval may follow this lead.

Page – Jealousy and mistrust are found with this card. Whether justified or not this jealousy is furious and intense. Observations may be misconstrued or spark dramatic events.

Coins / Pentacles

Ace – New foundations in life and material successes. A new line of work may be in store, new workplace or a raise. Potential gifts may arise from a reading with this card.

Two – This card represents drastic change, typically the old being exchanged for the new. This cycle can continue for a long time, but with this card we are seeing the drastic exchange of new and old ideas or practices.

Three – New careers or projects arise dramatically, maybe catching you off guard. This may be a direct result of the Two of Coins card and its exchange of ideas. You may find new work in an old or dying field.

Four – Building of infrastructure or foundations for specific use. Planning and preparing for new projects is in store and should be treated seriously if the fruits are to be harvested from this venture.

Five – This card signifies worry and concern. Anxious thoughts and debilitating depression may endure if left unchecked. This worry arises from worldly activities such as new projects or the testing of new ideas or inventions.

Six – Rewards for hard work come with this card. Accomplishments and attainment of goals are on the horizon. Recognition may be in store as well for the successes.

Seven – This card may bring failures and abrupt interruptions of the successes you've found. These failures may be in full swing or just seem like they are inevitable. Negative outlook and disheartening experiences are abound.

Eight – This card brings reparations and improvements to earthly troubles. It signifies the need for caring and repairing wounds and problems.

Nine – This card typically signals success and gain. Financial gains are in store to reward your hard work and patience. You may also find gains that are not money, but overall successes and material gains.

Ten – This card signifies wealth and hard earned recognition. You may be getting a raise or award for your work. You may be selling a business or finishing a big project and expecting a reward.

King – Practicality and hard work. Earthly affairs need tending to and require a business mindset to complete everything that needs to be done.

Queen – Kindness and affection come with this card. Earthly indulgences and romanticism are abound.

Knight – Hard work and commitment come with this card. Lack of imagination and lack of creative faculties may arise, but in return a good work ethic and stamina are coming.

Page – This card may signify transformation and drastic change. This transformation is coming quick and should not be fought against.

This is the end of the minor arcana, let's now move onto the major arcana. These cards are more complex than the minor arcana, their images are more complicated and seem to be less organized than the minor arcana.

0. Fool – This card represents curiosity and careless freedom. It is represented by the number zero for its carefree nature, spontaneously moving any direction heedlessly.

I. Magician – This card is indicative of consciousness and birth. Creative faculties used to manifest your desires and dreams are common influences related to this card.

II. High Priestess – This is the dark side of a powerful female archetype. Dark do not necessarily mean negative, but it can be at times. Intuition and powerful moon energy are indicative of this card.

III. Empress – This is the more inviting end of the spectrum for the powerful female archetype. Nurturing love and affection are found with this card. Maternal instincts and emotional joys are indicative of this card.

IV. Emperor – This card is representative of power over large groups and influential leadership. Whether good or evil this card builds civilizations and sets boundaries for large groups.

V. Hierophant – This card represents religious institutions and spiritual traditions. Occult and magical knowledge are governed by the Hierophant, who is skilled in the wisdom and practice of magic.

VI. Lovers – This complicated card is representative of connections, whether platonic or romantic. These connections are what holds the universe together. Passion and love is needed to strengthen these connections.

VII. Chariot – This card is representative of the combinations and relations of powers. A chariot is the combination of beast and man working together, how the powers are used is up to the driver. Strength and power of will is indicated by this card.

VIII. Strength – This card shows the balance of opposites, being capable of seeing this balance is a great skill to have. This strength is effective as both mental and physical strengths.

IX. Hermit – Deep contemplative thought and spiritual introspection are indicated with this card. Self-reflective practices like meditation are attributed to this card. The Hermit prefers being alone and working out big issues in his mind.

X. Wheel of Fortune – This card represents fate and destined events. Luck, fortune and coincidence all are housed within this card. Fruits of seeds sown throughout life are also attributed to this card.

XI. Justice – This card is based on fairness and justice itself. Personal, social and spiritual justice are all aspects of this card. This card values moral high grounds and balanced judicial systems.

XII. Hanged Man – Huge changes in life and in perspective are attributed to this card. Change is constant, subtle and sometimes drastic and obvious. All change is housed in this card.

XIII. Death – The first assumption for this card is negativity, but this isn't necessarily the case. Death of an addiction or bad relationship is positive. This card represents cycles and transformations of the greatest caliber.

XIV. Temperance – This card is indicative of patience and facing adversity in a calm manner. Alertness, foresight and attention to detail are all aspects of this card. This requires balance and great observation skills.

XV. Devil – Another card with assumed negative connotations, this card represents free will and freedom rather than the bad guy of the bible. This freedom of will is crucial to the human experience and our highest liberated state.

XVI. Tower – This card represents the destruction of solid boundaries and institutions. Laws are changed and taboos are broken. This may occur in entire nations or internally to the selfhood of man.

XVII. Star – This is the card of hope and faith. The stars have been guiding lights for humanity for millennia, offering insight and energy to the downtrodden or lost. This card is a savior during trying times.

XVIII. Moon – This card behaves like the moon. Fluid and mysterious, emotions and confidence are affected with this card. Looking into our shadow selves and dark sides may be beneficial.

XIX. Sun – This card represents energetic power and influence that sustains life. Vitality and essence are keywords here, at its most intense the sun can be able to burn or dehydrate our beings.

XX. Judgement – This car is indicative of time itself. Nobody can escape the confines of time, and judgement will come. How you influence your society and the role you play in life is indicated with this card.

XXI. World – This card is the final card in the tarot. It is indicative of an end goal that has been achieved. Finding you place in the world and finding love or a home can be related to this card.

History of the Tarot

The mysterious nature of the tarot doesn't stop with its extensive history. While we can assume cards in some form have been around for longer than the tarot, the tarot itself cannot be exactly pinpointed to a specific date in history. Many believe the tarot came about in popular society from nomadic cultures and cunning folk that traveled and made a living from their magical prowess. The official timeline claims that the cards came from Egypt into Europe, or at least cards of some sort made that journey. This was in the 14th century and even then the cards had similar suits as we use today.

The first actual documentation of Tarot is dated between 1440 and 1455 in Italy, this is the time we can begin to see trump cards and complex images added to the suited cards. There are written descriptions of tarot cards dawning images of Greek gods, natural scenes and even various species of birds. These tarot decks were hand painted so almost no decks from this time have been preserved. One of the oldest decks available now is the Sola-Busca tarot. This deck has very dark images with plenty of violent and unsettling scenes.

Eventually the printing press was created and cards could be made on a much larger scale. This enabled more durable decks with more consistent images. Tarot made its way around Europe with ease after his invention. The Tarot of Marseilles was one of the more popular decks we still use today, originating in Milan and finding itself present during today's magical revival. The early 20th century saw the creation of Aleister Crowley's THOTH Tarot, a deck that the master magician meticulously created with emotional images that are deeply symbolic. Much more popular and better suited for beginners is the Pamela Coleman-Smith deck. This deck is the most commonly used deck for the western world, it is often called the Rider-Waite deck, although Coleman-Smith's artwork is responsible for this deck's success.

Today there are so many decks to choose from that it can be overwhelming. Many beginners opt for the Coleman-Smith deck since it is easy to work with and essentially sets the standard for tarot decks nowadays. When choosing a deck it is good to consider what will work for you and what you are wanting. A deck with historical value in the magical community will have a distinct personality compared to one that is frogged themed. The images do hold power and if the images are not designed to impart wisdom or inspire thought, then they won't. This being said, a skilled reader can practice divination with a standard 52 card poker deck and yield great results. We need to keep in mind that not all the power is in the cards, our spiritual faculties and inherent intuitive powers play a major role as well.

Practicing Tarot

You can find almost infinite ways to use and read with a tarot deck. Many use it to answer specific questions, where others are using it to learn about themselves. Communing with spirits, divination, magical insight and advice are only a few popular ways to use the Tarot. But how do we go about this practice?

There are no set ways to use the tarot, you could shuffle the deck and draw one card. This won't be as specific as many like, but nonetheless and reading. You could ask a distinct question to the cards, then draw on card. This will be a more specific reading for the distinct question. You can devise your own reading system if you wish, or use traditional methods that have been practiced for millennia.

There are endless possibilities with tarot, you can literally ask the deck any questions and gain insight. It doesn't have to be spiritual questions, you can ask about your career or love life as well. Typically there are certain 'spreads' that Tarot readers lay out that add a needed complexity for insightful readings. These spreads are designed to give readings for specific aspects of life. However you go about it as your embark on your Tarot journey, keep in mind our favorite phrase, if it works, then it works.

Once you have a deck you will want to get to know it. Go through the cards and familiarize yourself with the images and numbers. Take note of your first impressions form these cards. This is sort of a calibration practice, go through each card and really feel out how the image affects you. Once you have gotten comfortable with your deck you can try a reading. You may read for yourself or read for another person. Always get another person's permission to read for them before spreading the cards.

When performing a reading it can be done spontaneously or planned out. For at home readings and ones that you prepare for it is recommended that you have a reading space to lay the cards. This can be your altar or a table with a special cloth over it. If this cloth is used only for tarot, then even better. It helps immensely to have a routine that you go through with a tarot reading. These rituals help you get into 'the zone' for a clear and concise reading. Many people light incense, dim the lights and set up candles for a reading. Clearing your mind is helpful as well, this can be achieved with mediation before the reading. It is also common practice to call upon spirits or planets to guide you through a successful reading.

It's best to find a practice that is suited to you and your goals. Just because a certain technique works for other people doesn't mean it will work for you. Take time to develop a practice that you are comfortable with and that is effective for your purposes. Let's look at some popular spreads to get familiar with. These spreads are perfect for beginners and are some of the most commonly used spreads today.

Celtic Cross

This is a very popular spread that is commonly used today and thought to be one of the best for beginners. You can ask any question or simply just throw the spread and read it. Here is the Celtic Cross spreads:

Draw the first card and place in front of you.

Draw the second card and place it across the first card.

Place the third card to the right of these two.

Place the fourth card below the first.

Place the fifth card above the first

Place the sixth to the left of the first.

Now draw four cards, one at a time and place them to the right hand side of card number three. These cards should be placed slightly above one another.

Each of these cards has a specific meaning and represents a certain aspect of life within the Celtic Cross spread. Numerology may come into play here if you want to add another level of complexity to the reading. Here are the general representations of the Celtic Cross spread:

1. This card is the overall situation in question.
2. This card is what is going to help or hurt the situation in question.

3.   This card represents subconscious influence, and your hidden desires.
4.   This card represents past situations that affect the question at hand.
5.   This card represents you conscious desire and how it affects the question.
6.   This card is represents where you are going currently.
7.   This card is your mindset and attitude toward the question.
8.   This card represents energetic influences.
9.   This card is revealing of things that are unknown to you at the present moment.
10. This card represents the inevitable outcome and connects with the number 5 card.

Love Spread

This spread is used for gaining insight into romantic situations as well as platonic ones. Anything related to love and connection can be inquired about using this spread. This spread is much simpler that the Celtic Cross. The Love spread is an easy six card spread. Ask anything you like about companionship or relationships in general can be read through this spread. Use it to learn about current affairs or future relationships.

Draw the first card and place is to the top left of your tarot table.

Draw the second and place it to the right hand side of the first card.

Draw the third card and place it to the bottom left hand side of the first card.

Draw the fourth card and place it on the right hand side of the third card.

Draw the fifth card and place it on the right hand side of the fourth card.

Draw the sixth card and place it below the fourth card.

Of these six cards that you have drawn each one has its own distinct insight into the question or relationship at hand. These specific aspects of the question can be read into via the spread you just threw. They are as follows:

1. This card is representative of yourself and how you are feeling at the moment.
2. This card represents how your partner feels about you at the moment.
3. This card represents you and your partner's loving connection.
4. This card represents that strengths of your connection.
5. This card represents weaknesses in your connection.
6. This card represents what needs to be attended to in the relationship and what needs to be accomplished to maintain the relationship.

Spread for Success

The following spread is used to gain insight into financial problems and problems you have being successful in any aspect of life. Although widely used for monetary insight, this spread can be used to learn about success in many other aspects of life as well. This card is similar to the love spread, but is a five card spread. You could potentially use this card for a love reading, but a six card spread is the best suited number for love and relationships, especially with 6's Venus attributes.

Draw the first card and place it in the middle of your tarot table.

Draw the second card and place it to the left hand side of the first card.

Draw the third card and place it on the right hand side of the first card.

Draw the fourth card and place it above the second card.

Draw the fifth card and place it below the second card.

Just as with the love spread each of these cards has a distinct connection with certain aspects of the question at hand. Take time to analyze each card and how it may be attributed to successful occurrences in your life.

1.   This card represents the obstacle that is at hand.
2.   This card represents the challenges the obstacle is comprised of.
3.   This card will reveal challenges that are hidden or you are not aware of.
4.   This card represents how new people or other variables in the situation can help you with your success and growth.
5.   This card represents what actions you need to take to find success for the obstacle at hand.

These card spreads are in no way the only spreads that are available to be used. You could just as easily design your own spread using numerology and astrology and get just as accurate of a reading. These three spreads are great for beginners since they are vague and universal enough to be applied to a wide variety of situations. When practicing with these techniques be sure to have a clear mind and listen intently to you intuition. This will give you by far the best results. This is certainly easier said than done, but with practice you can better get in tune with your deck. This is also where routines and rituals come into play. If you have a set ritual that you perform each time you have a serious reading your mind will be used to clearing during the routine and can be more easily emptied before throwing the cards.

CHAPTER 8
Forecasting And Divination

We have found that numerology, astrology and the tarot are all incredible arts the hold ancient and meaningful power when practiced successfully. There are many uses for these arts but one of the most sought after skills is the art of divination, also known as forecasting. This skill involves seeking insight into future events through the use of these art forms. While this may seem like science-fiction it is actually a much older concept than many are lead to believe.

Having the ability to peek into the future will yield great responsibility and power. This practice should not be taken lightly, we are working with forces that to this day are mysterious and unpredictable. It is fair to say that while these arts may help you see into future events, they don't particularly give you the opportunity to alter them. Instead you may better be prepared for them, being able to navigate them with ease.

There is no true way to know how or why these practices work but it is safe to say that it is not simply the art alone. These crafts allow us to use our human potential to a higher degree, acting as tools to commune with unseen forces and spiritual intelligences. Humans aren't taught that they have these powers and must now rediscover them, these arts may just be the first step to rebuilding our relationship with the spiritual realms.

Some of us may have already experienced some sort of foresight, imagine any time you're thinking of someone you haven't heard from in a while and then they suddenly call you or walk into the coffee chop you're sitting in. These instances are not mere coincidence but our minds tapping into future events. If numerology, astrology and tarot helps us tap into these powers, then all the more reason to practice them.

There are many forms of divination, from runes, tea leaf readings, dice readings and pendulums. For our intents and purposes we will focus on our three main practices we have discussed in this book.

What is Divination?

Forecasting and divination are practices that aim to find meaning in future events through the ritual use of tools and occult arts. As we mentioned there are many forms of divination but the three we are dealing with in this book are among the most popular in the western world. Numerology, astrology and tarot are forecasting systems that have cemented their place in popular culture as the go to practices for divinatory arts for beginners and adepts alike.

The potential that is attainable through these arts is exponential, but one should be cautioned against using these arts for evil of extremely selfish reasons. Rather these art should be focused on the spiritual progression of humanity and personal navigation of an unfair society. These techniques can offer both of these incredible powers with dedication and practice.

These systems can be great for personal use or to help others, either way you are honing your divination skills and becoming a more adept practitioner of these arts. We need to consider our reasons for using these techniques, it is not recommended that an individual haphazardly approach these practices, or practice them simply for fun or experimentation. The ancient arts are to be taken very seriously and approached with respect.

Historical use of Divination

Alexander the Great wrote detailed accounts of his encounter with oracles as he was making his way through Egypt. He even accounts the oracle of Amun predicting his rise and inevitable downfall. May Greek and Roman texts have accounts of oracles and prophecies, detailing the experiences of many people who witness the divinatory arts in progress and subsequently coming to fruition. While most of recent history has these arts under scrutiny for being 'evil' or governed by evil beings, we are seeing a new rise in the open practice of these arts. Even the Christian bible has its fair share of divinatory events.

Communicating with gods and spirits to gain insight in future events was at one time a very noble and respectable field of work until the powerful Christian church made the practices unlawful. Kings and Queens used seers and magicians to help make important decisions, most notable John Dee who was hired by Queen Elizabeth I to help with her astrological timing. Dee can be attributed with Elizabeth's success by some accounts. This incredible history cannot be ignored when we discuss divination and forecasting arts.

We may not be trying to rule an empire with our practices but we are exploring them and finding ways to commune with unseen forces or spirits. With these practices we can further explore the human experience and attempt to find more meaning in our personal lives, not to mention increase our chances of success in the 'real' world. Let's take a look at some distinct practices and the details on how to go about starting them.

Practice

There are a variety of ways to start a practice of forecasting and divination. Some students may be more adept than others at first, but all people are capable of using these arts to better themselves or help others. Consider anytime you've come across a divinatory practice. Perhaps you've seen a needle tied to a thread and then hovered above a pregnant women's belly to fore tell the sex of the baby, or perhaps you have driven past a palm reader's shop while traveling through the city. When these arts are found in popular culture they often get passed off as just for fun, but if performed properly and with care, they can reveal secrets about the true nature of reality. These secrets are some of the most invaluable gifts bestowed onto mankind.

Some people may be able to casually contemplate a subject and get a distinct vision of what's to come in the future, this is quite rare but not totally unheard of. For our purposes in this book we will assume that we are starting from the very beginning. Let's look into some preparatory techniques to prepare the mind for communication and insight through a divinatory practice.

Meditation

The practice of meditation has been mentioned a few times throughout this book. Many are familiar with a meditation practice but for those that aren't we can loosely define meditation as a mindfulness practice that aims to teach someone how to control their own thought patterns and emotions. Meditation is typically practiced sitting down and is often accompanied by breathing exercises, music, incense or certain imagery.

It is very safe to say that meditation is the simplest and most effective technique to improve your life in every way. When approach with an open heart and practiced on a regular basis, meditation can change every aspect of your life by changing your perspective and effectively allowing you to control the chaos of the human mind. Physically you master breathing techniques and learn to keep consistent breath, rather than erratic breathing that doesn't adhere to a pattern. Our minds improve as we really sit and observe what's happening in our minds and how to take control of the chaos.

We can find an infinite number of meditation techniques online and in various books, research this practice and find a technique that works for you. It's a common misconception that meditation is a religious practice. This simply isn't true. Meditation can come in many forms, religious or not. No religion invented sitting quietly to yourself and breathing. While this incredible and simple practice did reach popular culture in the western world by way of India, the mediational process has been found in all ancient cultures. These cultures utilized trance-like states induced by meditation to commune with spirits and even foresee future events.

For beginners in divinatory arts meditation is perfect for clearing the mind before a ritual offering or tarot spread. Trance like states and clear minds make it much easier to analyze your results while practicing these arts, and when you're successful you will absolutely know! This cannot be stressed enough, you will *feel* when you are successful. Meditation will help eliminate any distractions so you won't be confused able your success.

Below we will look at an effective meditation technique that is great for beginners. We will keep it simple and concise for our purposes in this book.

Simple Meditation Practice:

1. Sit quietly and be comfortable in a familiar place with very little distraction
2. Breath in as deep as you are comfortable with and exhale slowly, counting one.
3. Continue this for ten deep breaths and then count backwards down to one again.
4. Continue this until you no longer need to count, and you are just keeping the rhythm of the breath.
5. Notice how the thoughts disappear and you are only focused on breath.
6. Continue as needed until you are in a clear mindset.

This is as simple as it gets for meditation. Adding other things to keep the senses occupied come in handy to clear the mind as well. Many people opt for trance inducing music, incense and symmetrical imagery to help keep the mind clear form earthly distractions. Combining mediation with an astrology or tarot practice is the quickest way to find success and really learn what works best for you.

Fasting

Another technique from our ancient ancestors, fasting is a practice that has grown in popularity recently in fitness circles and magical circles alike. Restricting caloric intake can be a very transformative experience, not just physically, but spiritually. Our senses become heightened when our bodies are adjusting to lack of quick energy, this can make a trance like state easier to attain.

Fasting can be dangerous so you must do your research and approach the practice with respect. Listen to your body and certainly do not just starve yourself. Ease into these dietary changes by eating a raw food diet for days leading up to a fast, and of course drink plenty of water. Some fasting ideas include restricting calorie intake to less than 750 a day and also only ingesting fluids for a day. Any other practice beyond this should be researched extensively or referred to a physician for information about.

Yoga

This another practice that people misconceive as a religious practice. Not unlike meditation, yoga can be used by anyone regardless of spiritual knowledge or religion. Yoga is comprised of postures, movements and breath work that aims to unite the body and mind. Trance like states can be induced with this practice, and so it pairs nicely with meditational techniques.

Plenty of information on yoga can be found online, in books and classes. This practice is perfect to get in touch with your body and prepare your mind for meditational techniques and thus your divinatory practice.

Music

If you live in a noisy area where there is no peace or just have a problem blocking out sounds, music can help dramatically. If were focusing on clearing the mind some types of music may not be suitable. For trance inducing we need drone music or music that is very repetitive. Atmospheric music and nature sounds are great choices for our purposes.

Some cultures use mantras, or repetitive phrases that are sung or chanted. These mantras could be prayers or just one word. This technique is great for inducing trance and blocking out distracting thoughts or noises. One of the more popular mantras is resonating the OM sound repetitively, this sound is thought to be one of the most ancient sounds for mantras.

Some people choose to use apps or recordings of white noise for a trance inducing drone. This wall of noise will block out every sound and actually affects the brain in ways that encourage one pointedness and trance states.

The above preparatory practices aim to induce trance-like states so that you may better receive messages or insight while performing a divinatory art. By clearing the mind we can better filter out distractions from our own brains and receive the insight and information we are searching for. Developing a routine and ritual will only improve our forecasting skills.

These arts are very powerful and if used correctly can offer insight into the most mundane situations to the hidden secrets of life. Use what you have learned in all the previous chapters to create a practice that suits your schedule and lifestyle. In the following chapter we are going to take time and combine all these techniques into an example of a balanced ritual for beginners.

CHAPTER 9
How Numerology, Astrology And Tarot Are Connected

For the final chapter in this book we are going to look at the relationship between the three arts we have discovered and also provide an example of a ritual that includes everything we have learned. To reiterate, we can customize these practices to suit our preferences. You may want to start out with a simple numerological practice, or just get to know your tarot deck for a while, this is fine and when you're ready to add more to your practice you can refer to this guide for ideas. However you decide to begin your journey, listen to your heart and focus on the task at hand. You may not always be obviously successful, the nature of reality can be elusive, but know that all the time and effort will be worthwhile.

I'm sure you can see the small connections between numerology, astrology and tarot. They are all used for forecasting and divination, and they are all ancient practices as well. Numerology and numbers are embedded in every aspect of life. The stars and astrology have guided humanity for millennia. And the tarot can be representative of the other two arts in tangible and beautiful forms, some even believe that each tarot card has an astrological meaning. These connections are not coincidences, these arts aim to connect humans with the unseen forces, acting as tools to open our minds and hearts to the true nature of reality.

Since these arts are connected we can form a very effective practice by using one or more of the arts for our purposes. If you are drawn to any one of these practices you have already begun your practice in some sense. There are reasons you hold this book, they may not be clear now, but will be shown to you in the future.

Below we will give a detailed example of how these practices can be combined will all we have learned to form an easy and effective ritual. This ritual is by no means the only way to approach these arts. But for a beginner who is practicing on their own this is a great way to take your casual interest in the arts to the next step.

A Ritual Guide

First things first for this example. You need to know what your purpose is in performing this ritual. Are you needing more income or success in your career? Are you seeking love? Are you trying to find your place in the world? Perhaps you are set on rebuilding your relationship with spirits or other realms. There are many questions you may seek answers to, and the more complex the questions the more complex the answers will be. Once you have contemplated and established what exactly you are looking for, we can begin to plan our ritual.

For this guide we are going to use finding love our ultimate goal. This is a common reason why people seek these arts and rightly so, it's difficult to navigate the dating scene in our busy and technological age, improving our odds of meeting someone is going to help exponentially. There are hundreds of 'love spells' online and in books, these types of spells tend to get out of control and cause strange things to happen to people, so avoid these. The route we are taking is much more generalized and will help you find a suitable lover rather than directing a love spell at someone you're infatuated with.

Planning a Day

We will need to choose an auspicious day to perform this ritual. Choose a day that that is favored by Venus since Venus deals in matters of love. Look at your natal chart and see where your natal Venus is positioned. Also see where Venus is positioned in the current chart as well. You will want to choose a day where Venus is in a sign that it rules or when Venus is transiting your natal Venus. If Venus is positioned unfavorably in your chart or is retrograde in your chart then opt for a day when Venus is in the sign it rules. You may have to wait for Venus to reach these positions but be patient.

You will also want to look at the 7th house in your natal chart, this house governs love and relationships and there are planets placed there unfavorably you may need to work with them as well to balance any detrimental factors.

For our purposes we need to choose a Friday with Venus in Taurus or Libra. Find an online resource or use an app to see when the next perfect Friday will be. Once we have found that day we can mark our calendars that this is the 'big day'. Keep in mind that we will want to perform the ritual in the hour of Venus as well, so at sunrise, midday or sunset on the planned Friday. If you can find a Friday that is a number that relates to Venus, 6, 15, 24, then even better. Otherwise a date that syncs with your personal numerology will work as well.

If you have ample time to wait before this day use it wisely, perhaps develop a consistent meditation or yoga routine to better prepare your mind to be clear for the ritual day. Have a prayer to Venus ready if your wish as well. You can also spend this time doing tarot spread for love to see what may be good routes to take or good insight. For this example we will also need incense and green candles. Also gathering some suitable offerings for Venus are needed as well. Venus likes flowers, spring water, champagne and gourmet sweets.

If you do not have an altar space or a space dedicated to magical workings it is recommended to create one. Maybe just a corner in your room or a dedicated shelf. This area can be set up however you like, pictures of dead relatives, spiritual statues and art are great for altars. Make it nice and clean and have a nice spot for you to sit nearby. If you cannot create this space have a private location outdoors where this ritual can be performed.

The Ritual Day

Today is the day. You can fast today or days leading up to this if you wish, this can be viewed as an offering or sacrifice to Venus. Drink plenty of water this day and be mentally prepared. For our example we will be performing the ritual in the morning and in the evening during the hour Venus.

Get to your ritual space, and turn off any phones or electronics nearby and avoid technology if possible tis day. Be sure you are showered and clean, and the same goes for your ritual space. As the hour of Venus approaches be ready with your offerings and prayers. Go to your ritual space and sit quietly for a moment. Light a green candle, or six if you can, and lovingly place your offerings in or on the space. Use fancy containers for the offerings. If you have a prayer or poem ready say it out loud as if you are performing it to Venus.

After you have the offerings and prayers given to Venus then sit quietly in a meditative state, focus breathing and imagine the glyph of Venus in your mind as you clear your head. Listen for any communication from Venus or just anything that comes to you be very aware of. Remain in this position until you feel comfortable and balanced.

At this moment get your tarot deck and shuffle them, keeping a meditative mindset. Throw a love spread onto the table or ground in your ritual space and read the cards you have. This spread may give you reading direct from Venus or offer insight into what steps to take next, be open and aware.

After the tarot spread has been successfully read you can leave your ritual space. Leave the candles burning and leave the offerings. Let Venus know that she is fine to stay in the room and in your life as she sees fit.

Spend your day quietly and preferable alone, contemplating your ritual experience. As night falls we can repeat this ritual in the hour of Venus, leaving more offerings and candles, saying the same prayer and throwing a tarot spread. Essentially do the exact same sequence. As you lay down to sleep be very aware of your dreams. It is common for beginners to receive insight during dreams, dream states tend to have less earthly distractions so they are perfect for receiving important information from planets and spirits.

Post Ritual

The days after your ritual should be spent normally. Go about your business as usual, you can throw tarot spreads and do Venus rituals on Fridays as you wish, but it's not necessary to do them every Friday. Give the magic time and really pay attention to changes in your life. Sometimes things come to you that are not obviously results of your ritual, you may not even notice them until much later.

This ritual has laid the foundation of your new practice. You can use a similar ritual to contact any of the planets, just be sure to substitute offerings and candles that the particular planet will appreciate. This ritual is one of the more complicated and powerful practices that is suitable for beginners, keeping track of casual astrological timing and numerological syncs is recommended for smaller practices. Now that your journey has begun you may build it, alter it and listen to the forces at work. They may want some specific offering or need something from you, so be open and listen closely as true nature of reality whispers to you.

CONCLUSION

Thank you for making it through to the end of *Numerology*, let's hope it was informative and able to provide you with all of the tools you need to achieve your goals whatever they may be.

The next step is to further your practice and keep track of the results. You have officially started a spiritual practice that is going to change your life for the better, so congratulate yourself and maybe reach out to a magical community near you. There are many magical paths you can take, be wise on your journeys and use these newfound powers to improve your life and improve the world around you.

Numerology, astrology and tarot have been integral tools to humanity for longer than we will ever know. You are now reclaiming these arts to empower yourself as an individual. You are rebuilding relationships with the unseen forces that our ancestors lived for. Not only is this work going to help you live your life to the fullest, but it will also go a long way in reclaiming humanity's path as a natural and magical one. This is often called the 'great work'. As you navigate this world be honest and loving, share your experiences and reach out to like-minded people who may need assistance.

This book is dedicated to the beginner in these ancient arts and aims to help anyone who is seeking the unknown. It has come to you for a reason and now that you have finished reading you can refer back to it for any insight in your journey. Take this knowledge with you for the rest of your life. You will find that there is no aspect of living that isn't touched by these practices and that they are capable of things beyond belief and beyond science. We hope your journeys are successful and as always keep in mind, if it works, then it works!

Finally, if you found this book useful in any way, a review on Amazon is always appreciated!

DESCRIPTION

Have you ever wondered about the powerful art of numerology, astrology and tarot? Do you have a strong sense of spiritual curiosity? Then this book has found its way to you for a distinct reason. These ancient arts have been integral practices found in all cultures from all around the planet. Humans have used these practices to commune with nature and gain insight into unseen realms for all of written history and perhaps even before. In this book you will discover:

- The historical use of Numerology
- How to use numbers to navigate reality
- Learn your personal numerology
- The historical use of Astrology
- How to use the planets to improve your life
- Learn your personal astrological makeup
- The history of Tarot cards
- How to use Tarot cards and various tarot spreads
- How to combine these arts into a practice
- How to design and customize a ritual
- The importance of these arts as a role in humanity

If these powerful arts have ever made their way into your life or even your thoughts this is the beginner's guide for you. Find your calling and live your life to the fullest by communing with the true nature of reality. This book holds the beginning steps to take on your spiritual journey. Empower yourself and take control of your destiny!

www.ingramcontent.com/pod-product-compliance
Lightning Source LLC
Chambersburg PA
CBHW071501070526
44578CB00001B/402